TRADITION

CROSSCURRENTS

ISI Books' Crosscurrents series makes available in English, usually for the first time, new translations of both classic and contemporary works by authors working within, or with crucial importance for, the conservative, religious, and humanist intellectual traditions.

TITLES IN SERIES

Equality by Default, by Philippe Bénéton, trans. by Ralph C. Hancock

A Century of Horrors, by Alain Besançon, trans. by Ralph C. Hancock and Nathaniel Hancock

Critics of the Enlightenment, ed. and trans. by Christopher O. Blum

Icarus Fallen, by Chantal Delsol, trans. by Robin Dick

The Unlearned Lessons of the Twentieth Century, by Chantal Delsol, trans. by Robin Dick

Democracy without Nations? by Pierre Manent, trans. by Paul Seaton

TRADITION
CONCEPT AND CLAIM

Josef Pieper

TRANSLATED FROM THE GERMAN BY
E. Christian Kopff

WILMINGTON, DELAWARE

Pieper, Josef, 1904–1997.
  [Überlieferung: Begriff und Anspruch. English]
  Tradition: concept and claim / Josef Pieper; translated with an introduction by
  E. Christian Kopff.—1st English ed.—Wilmington, Del.: ISI Books, 2008.

    p. ; cm.
    (Crosscurrents)
    ISBN: 978-1-933859-54-5
    Originally published in German as: Überlieferung: Begriff und Anspruch
    (Munich: Kösel, c1970).
    Includes bibliographical references.

    1. Tradition (Philosophy) I. Kopff, E. Christian. II. Title. III. Title: Überlieferung.
    IV. Series: Crosscurrents (Wilmington, Del.)

B105.T7 P5413 2008   2007942689
148—dc22   0806

            English translation published in hardcover in the
            United States by permission of St. Augustine's Press:

                        ISI Books
              Intercollegiate Studies Institute
                    Post Office Box 4431
                 Wilmington, DE 19807-0431
                      www.isibooks.org

            Manufactured in the United States of America

CONTENTS

Sartre's anti-tradition and "scientific philosophy." "An increasingly empty seriousness" (Karl Jaspers) and "empty freedom" Viacheslav Ivanov). / IV. The true unity of mankind is based on participation in the sacred tradition.

"The only reason we are still alive is our inconsistency in not having actually silenced all tradition."

—Gerhard Krüger, *Geschichte und Tradition*

TRANSLATOR'S PREFACE

FOLLOWING SOME DIFFICULTIES arranging for appropriate translators for Pieper's books, Helen Wolff, the wife of publisher Kurt Wolff and his chief copy editor, exclaimed, "If I die early, put on my tombstone the words: Killed by translators."[1]

Naturally, a translator hopes that his efforts will give new life to the text he is preparing, not kill his copy editor or the work itself. When Pieper and his wife Hildegard translated C. S. Lewis's *The Problem of Pain*, he added an epilogue, "On Simplicity of Language in Philosophy."[2] He republished this epilogue in a volume of essays with the significant title, *Tradition as Challenge*.[3] In 1987 he translated part of it as his acceptance speech for the Ingersoll Awards in Chicago.[4]

The importance of simple language for philosophy and poetry had interested Pieper since his days as a student. Young Pieper read a passage from a fashionable author, the Danish Lutheran Søren Kierkegaard, to a favorite teacher, who responded, "Not bad! But—these are store-bought pastries. You need bread, preferably dark rye bread." He recommended Aquinas's commentary on the prologue to John's Gospel. The eager schoolboy discovered that, while Aquinas's vocabulary was not especially difficult for anyone with a good classical education, the thought was challenging. The use of simple words did not entail a simple-minded exposition of the ideas involved.[5]

Personally, I find Pieper's language lively and idiomatic rather than simple or plain, perhaps because many of his books were first composed as lectures. His arguments, however, are indeed challenging, and in the course of making them, Pieper confronts major figures from the entire history of Western thought and beyond.

Pieper consistently followed a strategy of presenting important ideas unpretentiously. A translator is tempted to frustrate this strategy by making the vocabulary of his books match his serious themes. Translators sometimes render key terms by their Latinate equivalents, whereas Pieper used ordinary German words. (In their defense, English usage often affords no idiomatic alternative to a Latinate term.) His early book *Vom Sinn der Tapferkeit*[6] (On the Meaning of Bravery) was translated as the Latinate *Fortitude*,[7] an unusual substitute for the more common "bravery" or "courage." In that book, Pieper argues that bravery is an important virtue and that we need to talk about it straightforwardly, neither demoting it from the classical cardinal virtues nor forgetting that in the classical tradition it ranked third after intelligence and justice and thus "depends on justice." These were important points to make in 1934, when the book was published. Bravery was then being denigrated by pacifist rhetoric, on the one hand, and exalted by the propaganda of the incumbent German government, on the other. The use of highfalutin' language would have undermined Pieper's attempt to recover the traditional understanding of bravery, which was not only sound philosophy, but also common sense.

As for "fortitude," as soon as the English adjective is needed, "brave" appears. This variation of theological and ordinary language is not found in Pieper's German—quite the contrary. *Tapfer* and *Tapferkeit*, brave and bravery, resound like the strokes of a hammer throughout the text. Pieper does not use even the Latin *fortitudo* until the last chapter.

The opposite is true of the central concern of *Tradition*, where the words *Überlieferung* and *Tradition* are used interchangeably to emphasize the pervasive reality that underlies these two Germanic and Latinate words for the same important concept.

Pieper pursued a similar strategy in the format of his publications. They have now been reprinted in the impressive hardbound complete works edited by Berthold Wald for Felix Meiner Verlag.[8] They originally appeared, however, as unpretentious little "paperbacks" with plain yellow covers and could be slipped into a coat pocket or handbag to read on the train or bus. Pieper was pleased to find the "Great Books" available in paperback when he came to the United States in 1950. He was a little shocked, however, when he saw a translation of Aristotle's *Poetics*, published by Henry Regnery; it sported on its cover a banner promising the prospective reader the answer to the question, "Why see sad movies?" Pieper was told, "The only chance the average American has to see a tragedy is in the movie theater. So we ended up talking about 'sad movies.'"[9]

Pieper tells his readers his sources, but he was not fussy about using up-to-date texts or complete references. I have cited standard critical editions and English translations when they exist. Usually, however, I have modified them to suit Pieper's text. Readers who are interested in the context of passages he cites can find it by using my notes. When Pieper quotes German translations from works published in other languages and for which an English version exists, I have omitted his references and cited only the English. I made an exception for Jung's *Psychology and Religion*, which was originally a series of lectures delivered in English at Yale, because I thought the German translation might reflect Jung's intentions. The quotations from Gabriel Marcel are from a lecture given originally in German at Münster, where Pieper taught. My own additions to text and notes are marked by brackets. Pieper used brackets in his rather idiosyncratic punctuation, but in this translation they are used only to mark my textual interpolations and notes or his additions to passages he quotes.

Within the constraints he set himself, Pieper wrote interesting and lively German. His best literary effects are hard to transfer into English. One example in *Tradition* is clearer to someone listening to his recorded lecture, "What Can Tradition Mean to Us Today?"[10] Pieper places a reference to Pascal's "Introduction to a Treatise on the Void" near the beginning of both book and talk. He consistently translates "void" and "vacuum" as *das Leer*, the empty. Near the end of the book he quotes from Karl Jaspers and Viacheslav Ivanov sentences where the word "empty," *leer*, is significant. His argument is framed by the emphatic repetition of the German word *leer*, which to my ears evokes the feeling of emptiness better than the heavy English word "empty." Even the language of his notes can be interesting. In note 6 to chapter 2 Pieper writes of what August Deneffe wrote in *seiner sehr klaren und klärenden Studie*. My English rendition—"in his very clear and enlightening study"—gives the sense without reproducing the verbal wit. In most cases I have been satisfied to write idiomatic and clear English explanations of Pieper's meaning.

I do not think Pieper would have objected. He knew English well and was aware that it tends to be drier and more matter-of-fact than German. In his essay "What Does 'Christian West' Mean?"[11] he comments, "When in discussions with Anglo-Saxons *abendländische Kultur* abruptly and unexpectedly becomes 'Western civilization,' I feel as though the words were being twisted around in my mouth and that the best and most important part of what I meant was knocked out of my hand by a trick." This trick, however, was the simple act of translating German into the "ruthless sobriety" of English. Despite his immediate emotional response, in the end he decides that translating his thoughts into English is a good thing, because it involves a "test of authenticity and simplicity." "It is probably very healthy to be reminded that the German word for 'evening,' *Abend* here [in the word *abendländische*] refers simply to the compass point where the sun goes down, that is, to the west." In deference to this point I have usually chosen to compose straightforward explanations over attempts to reproduce Pieper's evocative German. Even someone who does not know German may get a feeling for Pieper's irreproducible delight in language from the following sentence from chapter 2:

> *To hand down*, tradieren, überliefern, heißt nicht einfach: jemandem etwas geben, bringen, mitteilen, aushändigen. Es heißt vielmehr: jemandem etwas zuvor in die eigene Hand Gelangtes, etwas Eingehändigen; etwas Bekommenes und Überkommenes mitteilen; etwas Empfangenes weitergeben—damit es wiederum empfangen und weitergeben werde.

Pieper cites the *Summa Theologiae* of Thomas Aquinas from the Marietti edition, *Summa Theologiae* I–IV (Turin/Rome 1948–50), which reprints the text of the Leonine edition, the standard critical edition, which I have used and cited for the *Summa* and other works by Thomas. Details are given in the bibliography. Pieper cited passages from the *Summa* in numerical form—for example, II, II, 2, 7 ad 3, that is, the Second Part of the Second Part, *quaestio* [question] 2, *articulus* [article] 7, answer to the third objection. I and other translators follow him in this convention. Pieper always writes *Summa Theologica*, although both the Leonine edition and the Marietti reprint call it *Summa Theologiae*.

In translating the table of contents and arranging the subheadings, I have shown considerable, but not total, respect for the first edition of *Überlieferung*. In a few places I have drawn upon Pieper's 1957 lecture, "On the Concept of Tradition," when I thought the expression was clearer or I understood it better.

In 2006, Ignatius Press published a translation by Roger Wasserman of the third volume of Pieper's *Werke*, edited by Bernhard Wald, which includes a reprinting of *Überlieferung*.[12] Readers may observe the differences and similarities.

I have drawn upon the suggestions and advice of many people while working on this translation, including Jacob Neuhaus, David Whalen,

Adrian del Caro, and Thomas Hollweck. My warm thanks go to the editors and staff of ISI Books for encouraging this translation and seeing it through the press. My apologies for those I have forgotten. They are not responsible for the use I made of their help.

E. Christian Kopff
Boulder, Colorado
August 2007

TRANSLATOR'S INTRODUCTION

REFLECTIONS ON TRADITION AND THE PHILOSOPHICAL ACT IN JOSEF PIEPER

I

I saw Josef Pieper once, the evening of November 5, 1987, at the Drake Hotel in Chicago, where he had come to receive the Ingersoll Award in Scholarly Letters from the Rockford Institute. He was smiling and unprepossessing. His talk, published as "On Clarity," was itself clear and arresting.[1]

The press paid most attention to the other recipient, Mexican poet Octavio Paz, who would go on to be awarded a Nobel Prize, despite his unconcealed monarchism. (The other monarchist to be awarded the Ingersoll was French novelist Jean Raspail.) Quite a few Catholics attended the awards banquet, however, out of a desire to see the author of *Leisure: The Basis of Culture*.[2] Thomas Fleming, the editor of *Chronicles*, introduced Pieper and told the audience that he had first read Pieper when he was loaned *Leisure* by "one of my Greek teachers,"[3] probably Kenneth Reckford, a classics professor and popular undergraduate teacher at Chapel Hill who often talked about

Pieper. *Leisure* is Pieper's best-known book in America, but many of his books—on Plato, scholasticism, Thomas Aquinas, the seven virtues— have been translated and reviewed respectfully.

There are interesting parallels between *Tradition* and *Leisure*. The modern world pays lip service to both, but usually has little use for either. Frank moderns express scorn for them, as Ernst Jünger does for leisure and Mikhail Gershenzon for tradition. Pieper reminds us of the importance attached to them by great ancient philosophers, like Plato and Aristotle, argues that they are essential for a fulfilled human life, and shows that, despite all the secular advantages we derive from them, they rest on a religious basis. When they are separated from religion, or if religion loses its central place in society, both leisure and tradition become deformed and derailed from their main functions. Either there is no time for real leisure, or what leisure remains is turned into an activity, instead of a time for contemplation and reflection. Either we lose touch with tradition, or it becomes a set of meaningless rituals. "The man who diverges from the traditional is a victim; the one who does not is a slave," as Nietzsche wrote.[4]

Pieper found the theme of *Tradition* important enough to return to it in different formats over the years. Key ideas appeared in the final chapter of *Was heißt Philosophieren* (1947), translated in 1952 with *Leisure* as *The Philosophical Act. Tradition*, published in 1970, is a revision of a lecture he gave more than a decade earlier, as he explained in a paragraph that appears before the endnotes of the 1970 text:[5]

> In the preceding text thoughts have been borrowed which the author delivered in January 1957 before the Rheinisch-Westfälische Akademie der Wissenschaften (which was called in those days the Arbeitsgemeinschaft für Forschung). The lecture, which has since gone out of print, was published in its scholarly series together with the discussion which followed it under the title, *On the Concept of Tradition.*[6]

Pieper devoted several shorter essays to this theme, including "Tradition in a Changing World"[7] and "Threatening and Preserving Tradition,"[8] which he recorded as "What Can Tradition Mean to Us Today?"[9] Although Pieper wrote in 1970 of borrowing "thoughts" from the 1957 talk, the structure of these works and even the words are the same or similar. The 1970 version takes notice of responses to the discussion that followed the 1957 talk, criticisms of his work, and other significant writings on tradition.

II

I would like to devote a few pages to other thinkers who have dealt with tradition. Pieper mentions Karl Jaspers and Hans-Georg Gadamer, who take tradition seriously but do not discuss Pieper, and Jürgen Moltmann and Odo Marquard, who contest Pieper's ideas. These thinkers, philosophers, and theologians expound their thoughts in such subtle and differentiated ways that it is impossible to explain or respond to their arguments in a brief essay. Still, a few comments on their work and the book's intellectual background may be helpful in understanding what Pieper was trying to accomplish.

Pieper's discussion of Moltmann, an important Lutheran theologian, should be supplemented with Pieper's essay, "Future without a Past and Hope without a Foundation?"[10] There he argues that it is dangerous for theologians to concentrate too exclusively on the Christian virtue of hope, which needs the sacred tradition to provide it with content and meaning. "A future without a past is null and void. And a hope without a foundation—without one that exists before hope and us as well—is just another name for despair."

Pieper is dismissive of Theodor Adorno's "Theses on Tradition," a dialectical attempt to confront the modern world's simultaneous lack of and need for tradition. The end of Adorno's section 4 echoes *Tradition*'s epigram from Gerhard Krüger and the quotation from Leszek Kolakowski near the book's end. "Tradition today," Adorno writes, "poses an irresolvable contradiction. None is present and none can be conjured up, but when every tradition has been erased, so begins the descent into barbarism" (*so beginnt die Einmarsch in die Unmenschlichkeit*).[11] Pieper's criticism of Adorno's lack of precision may be a reference to his failure to distinguish different types of tradition. It is misleading for Pieper to suggest that Adorno was an uncritical rationalist. *The Dialectic of Enlightenment*, which Adorno wrote with Max Horkheimer, describes how the success of the Enlightenment project, with all its attendant benefits, involves a narrow instrumental rationality (*Zweckrationalität*) and a bureaucratic state and economic regime that increasingly and inevitably limit human freedom and frustrate human fulfillment.[12]

Pieper objects testily to Marquard's description of his views. No doubt Marquard was wrong to attribute to him the view "Philosophy is the practice of tradition," since Pieper had explained, "Strictly speaking, the philosophizer, while he is philosophizing, is neither handing down tradition nor interpreting tradition."[13] For Pieper, philosophizing begins with wondering at, and goes on to ask questions about, the whole of reality, not just tradition. He does think, however, that sacred tradition was historically important in the creation of philosophizing and remains indispensable for its continuing vitality.

III

No matter how philosophy began, contemporary academic philosophers are often resolutely hostile to tradition and even feel a calling to subject traditional views to a withering critique. In the field of moral philosophy, for instance, Kant's categorical imperative, with its demand that all valid moral principles must be universalizable, is often explained as meaning that philosophers are exempt from dealing with the moral traditions of mankind. The intellectual task is challenging but the rule is simple. Can we will a moral principle to be a universal law for everybody, including ourselves, yes or no? Pieper believed that confronting moral and religious traditions is an essential part of philosophizing, as is clear from his practice in his books on the seven virtues and his arguments in the last chapter of *The Philosophical Act*.[14]

Gadamer's *Truth and Method* restored tradition to an honorable place in German scholarship as part of his strategy of seeking to prevent the marginalization of the humanities before the prestige of scientific methodologies. Gadamer's scholarly style differs from Pieper's in a number of significant ways; for example, he wrote scholarly monographs and academic articles rather than the unpretentious little books Pieper preferred. But the similarities are also significant. Both men confront modern problems without losing sight of the great ancient philosophers, especially Plato and Aristotle, or the Christian tradition. In Gadamer's classic essay "The Relevance of the Beautiful," for instance, there is a discussion of the role of the symbol in art in which he attempts to clarify the issue by discussing both Aristophanes' speech from Plato's *Symposium* and the debate between the Protestant Reformers Luther and Zwingli on Christ's Real Presence in the Lord's Supper.[15] Similarly, Pieper often develops his thinking by turning to Plato, Aristotle, and Aquinas. In fact, he discusses this same speech of Aristophanes several times, including in *The Philosophical Act*.[16]

In 1970, when *Tradition* was published, it was common to hear academic philosophers in American universities distinguish between colleagues who "do philosophy" and those who "do history of philosophy." Real philosophers did not need to attend to the past of their own discipline, never mind sacred tradition. That situation was soon to change. John Rawls and Charles Taylor showed how relevant and even essential Kant (in Rawls's case) and Hegel (in Taylor's) were for contemporary discussions.[17] Of course, Rawls's *A Theory of Justice* suggested a way to escape from the traditions and historical forms of actual societies. At the time it was thought an accident that Taylor's book not only discussed Hegel's critique of Kant, but also suggested valid responses to Rawls's neo-Kantian vision. Still the history of philosophy suddenly began to seem a lot more relevant.

Rawls's further work indicates that he can be characterized as a creative philosopher who used the work of a major figure in the history of philosophy to attempt to liberate political thought, at least, from the trammels of the past. Charles Taylor is a more complicated figure. His extensive publications after his *Hegel* have investigated and explored important modern themes by employing a rigorous and up-to-date philosophical methodology, with only hints that there might be a spiritual component to understanding the issues of modernity. His work was very influential in laying a philosophical basis for the communitarian movement. (Taylor was also an active participant in Canadian politics.) In 1996, he delivered the Marianist lecture at the University of Dayton.[18] The lecture is usually given by prominent Catholic scholars who use it to discuss the relationship between their faith and scholarship. On March 8, 2005, Taylor lectured at the Josef Pieper Stiftung in Münster as recipient of the first Josef Pieper Preis, given for "outstanding philosophical writings on the European and Christian picture of humanity."[19] Taylor began the lecture by expressing his admiration for Pieper's work as a philosopher, with which he felt a deep affinity, because of Pieper's idea, expressed in *The Philosophical Act*, of practicing philosophy in a contrapuntal relationship with Christian theology.

With Alasdair MacIntyre's *After Virtue* (1981) and his later books,[20] the concept of tradition became the subject of serious and detailed research and debate in Anglo-Saxon philosophy. MacIntyre's thought is too subtle and learned (and at times just too complicated) to allow a satisfactory comparison with Pieper here, but it is worth noting that an important theme of MacIntyre's work has been to explain the contemporary crisis in moral philosophy by arguing that coherent discussion takes place only within traditions. Debate between traditions is difficult, and attempts to carry on fruitful discourse outside of any particular tradition or tradition in general are doomed to futility. Not all traditions are equally successful in making sense of the past or in solving contemporary problems, but MacIntyre has argued that there are no extra-traditional criteria by which individual traditions can be judged.

McIntyre's analysis has led to charges that ultimately his position is as relativistic as the moderns he criticizes so memorably.[21] Pieper may have a contribution to make here, since he posits the original unity of the sacred traditions of mankind. Although the original sacred tradition was shattered and scattered by the passage of time or a traumatic Tower of Babel event, that original unity and coherence and the traces the sacred tradition has left in cultures, myths, and the human psyche itself provide reasons to hope that different human traditions can find in their shared origin in sacred tradition common ground for discussion and debate.

IV

The tension between reason and tradition did not begin with modernity. Pieper's books on scholasticism and Aquinas show how central this tension was to medieval thought. Anselm, for instance, is a great philosopher for whom human reason alone was capable of demonstrating God's existence and other important truths, although he accepted what the Bible says as true. For Pieper, Aquinas represents a reaction against this strain of scholastic philosophy, since he sees that reason and tradition, *ratio* and *auctoritas*, need one another. Reason questions and evaluates human traditions, but it accepts and builds on sacred tradition. Aquinas devotes much of his work to showing the fundamental compatibility of Christianity with Aristotle's philosophy (and the neo-platonic tradition, too). In his *Summa* he subjected Aristotle to a systematic re-platonizing. (MacIntyre's analysis of Aquinas is distinctively different but reaches similar conclusions.)[22]

Pieper's interest in Aquinas went back to his schoolboy years at the Gymnasium Paulinum in Münster, but he did not feel comfortable being described as a Thomist and could not give a satisfactory answer to requests from American colleagues to identify the "school" of neo-Thomism to which he belonged. He explained in an essay titled "Philosophy in His Own Words" that "it was simply impossible to place me under the rubric 'Thomism' or 'Neo-scholasticism,'" despite his lifelong interest in Aquinas. ("The one time, however, I felt I was characterized in a really mistaken fashion was when I was introduced at a guest lecture at the University of Chicago as 'a Christian existentialist.'")[23]

Naturally, Pieper casts a cold eye on the tendency of twentieth-century neo-Thomism to privilege abstraction over historical tradition. He refers to "the Cartesian-hued rationality" of French neo-Thomism.[24] (References to Descartes in Pieper are rarely complimentary.) He regarded the scholars associated with that movement as engaged in a mistaken return to Anselm and the German Enlightenment philosopher Christian Wolff.[25] I think he would have sympathized with Thomas Fleming's critique of the fate of the doctrine of "subsidiarity" under neo-Thomism:

> Brilliantly simple in conception, subsidiarity shares a fatal flaw with Catholic natural law theory: a rationalistic and antiempiricist bias. By stating the principle in abstract—rather than concrete and historical terms—Pius XI left it exposed to misuse. Almost inevitably, the modernizing John XXIII turned subsidiarity on its head and used it to justify state ownership and even intervention into national and local affairs by "the public authority of the world community."[26]

In the 1930s, Pieper wrote frequently about the encyclical to which Fleming refers, Pope Pius XI's *Quadragesimo Anno* (1932), but he was more concerned with the proper role of private property and the future of the working class. His brief discussion of subsidiarity argues that this principle does not imply a purely "night watchman" role for the state.[27] After World War II he was drawn to other themes.

For Pieper, Plato's writings provide indispensable help in interpreting the sacred tradition, and Plato and Aristotle share a common philosophical mission. In his youth, the most influential interpretation of Aristotle was Werner Jaeger's, who saw Aristotle as developing in stages from a faithful student of Plato's at the Academy (367–47 B.C.) into the fully distinctive Aristotle of his years at his own research institution, the Lyceum (335–23 B.C.).[28] Pieper believed that "the most exciting conclusion of Jaeger's Aristotle book"[29] is that "[t]he history of his development shows that behind his metaphysics, too, there lies the *credo ut intelligam*."[30] He even writes that Boethius's vision of "Aristotle the Platonist" "has been proven to be authentic by the research of Werner Jaeger."[31] Today, under the influence of G. E. L. Owen and Wolfgang Kullmann, scholars investigate how Aristotle formulated his own responses to distinctively platonic questions.[32] As MacIntyre writes, "I understand Aristotle as engaged in trying to complete Plato's work, and to correct it precisely insofar as that was necessary in order to complete it."[33] Pieper's interpretation of Aristotle, which he assumed consistently and without a polemical posture, seems prescient. In general, Pieper shared the opinion of John M. Rist, that, if Christians are to take advantage of the contributions of classical thought, "we should find that is not just any philosophical framework within which Christian thinkers can work, but a version of the system of Plato, adapted and reformed particularly in the areas of what we should now call theory of action by the much more detailed labours of Aristotle, while still, in respect of the importance of a providential and transcendent God, in essence and in core platonic."[34]

Rist and Pieper are not the only contemporary thinkers convinced that Plato can still serve as a model for philosophizing. Arbogast Schmitt's *Modernity and Plato*[35] explores the problems modern thinkers have faced because they have ignored Plato and platonism. He begins with a clear-sighted analysis of the fashionable tendency to see a "paradigm shift" (Germans speak of *die Wende*) in many different areas and problems, so that "after [X] everything is different," with the result that scholars and thinkers can safely ignore examining or learning about that which preceded the selected date or event. Here Pieper's work is a healthy corrective, since in almost every book he turns to Plato, Aristotle, and Aquinas not as figures possessing incidental insights of interest, but as models of how to think about the most important problems. Schmitt's critique of the many aspects of modernity that suffer from ignoring Plato is thorough and important. In any case, it may be no coincidence that Rist, from a Christian perspective, and Schmitt, from a secular one, both see Plato as an indispensable resource in confronting the intellectual, ethical and political challenges facing today's world.

V

Although Pieper emphasized the human duty to learn and accept the sacred tradition in order to hand it down undiminished and unchanged, he was well aware that taking sacred tradition seriously leads to creativity and even innovation.

First, the duty to transmit sacred tradition uncorrupted cannot be performed successfully unless the recipients of tradition come to understand its truth and importance. There has been and must be a considerable amount of creativity in this activity, as shown by the range and longevity of religious art, music, and literature in both high and low culture. This continuing mission involves different tasks in every generation. Sometimes the task will involve preserving customary words and rituals, but not always. "True consciousness of tradition liberates from the conservatisms."

Sacred tradition has also played an essential role in the formation and maintenance of traditions not directly concerned with preserving it, like philosophy. Historically, sacred tradition provided the basis for the beginning of philosophy. "The great originators of Western philosophy, on whose thought it largely lives, Plato and Aristotle, not only found and recognized a 'traditional' interpretation of the world alive and vigorous—they accepted it as their starting point when they began to philosophize."[36]

The importance of sacred tradition does not end with its role in the origins of philosophy. Pieper rejects the modernist metanarrative in which at a certain stage philosophy moves beyond tradition and replaces it with critical thought. On the contrary, philosophy survives by interacting in contrapuntal fashion with sacred tradition. Philosophy confronts the entire world, not sacred tradition alone, which is the task of theology. To desert the sacred tradition, however, or to ignore it, leads to the death of philosophy, as Pieper says in *Tradition* and in his lectures published as *Scholasticism*:

> The very moment someone engaged in philosophizing ceases to take his bearings from sacred tradition, two things happen to him. First he loses sight of his true subject, the real world and its structure of meaning, and instead talks about something entirely different, namely, philosophy and philosophers. Second having forfeited his legitimate hold on the only authoritative tradition, he must illegitimately and (by the way) vainly seek support in the mere facts handed down, in randomly chosen historical "material."[37]

VI

I believe that Pieper's insights on the dependence of true philosophy on tradition also hold true of science. Pieper follows Pascal in contrasting fields where tradition is decisive, like theology, and others where it is irrelevant, like physics, where results are achieved by experiments and logic. Tradition, of course, does not play the same role in physics and the other natural sciences that it does in theology, but it does play a role nonetheless. As MacIntyre has perceived, "All reasoning takes place within the context of some traditional mode of thought, transcending through criticism and invention the limitations of what had hitherto been reasoned in that tradition: this is as true of modern physics as of medieval logic."[38] For Pieper, Plato and Aristotle began from the sacred tradition as they knew it. Thales, the first scientist, was probably inspired by Babylonian sacred tradition.[39] The role of mathematics in science begins with the ancient Greek guru and mystic Pythagoras.[40] Eugene Wigner called its effectiveness "unreasonable";[41] Pieper might have preferred the term "unfathomable."[42]

Scientists learn facts but also—sometimes implicitly—a worldview: the world they study is a unity that is rational and comprehensible.[43] These assumptions are matters of faith which must be accepted before applying critical intelligence to specific problems. To use Pieper's term, within the tradition of science they are *tradita*. Accepting them and relying on them, scientists come up with original discoveries and hypotheses, which must be checked by experiments and arguments. Some of the great debates of science, between Galileo and Kepler, for instance, are about *tradita*, not observation and experiment. We find a more recent example in Einstein's letter to Max Born (December 6, 1924), in which he expressed his reservations about the Copenhagen interpretation of quantum physics. "Quantum mechanics is certainly impressive. But an inner voice tells me that it is not yet the real McCoy. The theory has been very productive, but it does not really bring us any closer to the Old Man's secret. I, at any rate, am convinced that *He* does not play dice."[44] The inner voice that supported Einstein's conviction that the universe is not random comes from tradition, not observation and experiments. It echoes *Physics* II.8, where Aristotle criticized Empedocles' view that randomness could lead to a world that appeared designed. (Aristotle's comments suggest the relevance of Einstein's *bon mot* to neo-Darwinism.)

To show that "tradition has no place in science," Pieper quotes Aquinas's teacher, Albertus Magnus. According to Pieper, Albert wrote that the relevant criterion for deciding whether a dolphin was a fish or a mammal was observation of dolphins, not Aristotle's opinion.

Experimentum solum certificat in talibus (In such matters experience alone brings certainty). There are several problems with Pieper's discussion.

The first one is pedantic. The Latin quotation comes from Albert's work on plants and has nothing to do with dolphins. Pieper gives the correct context of Albert's Latin in his book on *Scholasticism*: "Albert is talking about the plants he is about to discuss."[45] Pieper's memory has confused this passage with Albert's discussion of whales (not dolphins) in *De animalibus* 24.1.23: "These are the facts which we have experienced concerning the nature of whales. We are passing over the things which the ancients wrote, since they do not find agreement among the experts."[46] Although his references are confused, Pieper's general point about Albert is correct. Albert did understand that his ancient sources were sometimes in error and checked them against his own observation and those of other experts. (For a balanced discussion of his work as a scientist, see Lynn Thorndike, *A History of Magic and Experimental Science*.)[47]

The role of tradition in science has been the subject of extensive research, beginning with Michael Polanyi and Karl Popper in the 1940s.[48] Although Pieper usually kept up with the latest research, or, as with the relationship between Plato and Aristotle, was even "ahead of his time," in this case he did not acknowledge the scholarly discussions of science and tradition, which have continued after the publication of *Tradition* in such works as Werner Heisenberg's essay "Tradition in Science" and the discussion of "The Presence of the Past in Works of Science and Scholarship" in Edward Shils's book *Tradition*.[49] This research is detailed and sophisticated. Let me mention a few important aspects.

Scientists reason about observable phenomena. The reasoning itself, however, and the questions they ask are traditional. Aristotle is an integral part of that tradition. It was Aristotle who argued that the study of animate life, what we today call biology, is just as worthy of serious study as physics.[50] The issue of classification—the question

Albert is discussing—goes back to Aristotle's practice.[51] Even the role of observation in controlling theories and opinions was formulated by Aristotle.[52]

The methods of theology are those of traditional philosophy. Its subject is sacred tradition, which plays the same role in theology that observation does in biology. In his essay "What Is a Church?" Pieper discusses the doctrine of the Real Presence of Christ in Holy Communion, "who, as someone really present, unites himself, in the bread and wine, with the faithful celebrants at the Lord's Supper." He comments, "I know that such claims appear quixotic and incredible to every normal, natural understanding. And I myself would not take the word of any theologian, no matter how brilliant, that they are true, if I did not know that they have been vouched for by a 'word of God.'"[53]

In biology, Albertus Magnus privileged observation over the word of any philosopher, no matter how brilliant. In theology, Pieper privileged the Word of God over any theologian, no matter how brilliant. The Real Presence, by the way, was the most important issue that separated Luther and Zwingli during the Reformation. Zwingli used reason and experience to make his case. Luther's argument came from the Bible. He wrote on the table that separated them, "*hoc est corpus meum.*" *Sermo dei solum certificat in talibus.*[54]

Pascal, of course, was right to insist that physics and theology differ distinctively in their criteria for confirmation and falsification of theories and hypotheses. The scientific problems that he studied, however, encouraged him to deny tradition any role in physics. This was not true of all scientists in the seventeenth century. In the "General Scholium" he added to the second edition of *Principia*, Isaac Newton wrote, "This most elegant system of the sun, planets and comets could not have arisen without the design and dominion of an intelligent and powerful being. . . . He rules all things, not as world soul but as lord of all. And because of this dominion he is called Lord God *Pantokrator*."[55]

Strictly speaking, the philosophizer, while he is philosophizing, and the scientist, while he is engaged in science, are neither handing down tradition nor interpreting tradition. Both science and philosophy, however, have a common origin in ancient Greek thinkers who were confronting sacred tradition. Throughout history philosophers and scientists have returned to sacred tradition as part and parcel of their mission. Even rejecting sacred tradition involves confrontation and influence, as Pieper observes about Jean-Paul Sartre, and as we might say about Richard Dawkins, for instance. And not all contemporary philosophers and scientists reject sacred tradition. Josef Pieper's words on the necessity of tradition have something to say to them and to the rest of us.

CHAPTER 1

IS TRADITION ANTI-HISTORICAL?

IN THE BEWILDERINGLY diverse web of the complicated process we call "history" we can distinguish countless different strands. Tradition is one, but it is not only fundamentally different from all the rest. The first impression it makes is of something completely odd and inappropriate. You might ask whether tradition is not downright anti-historical.

I

The most visible strand is certainly the constant progress of scientific research into the natural world and mankind and, conditioned and inspired by this, the increasingly thorough exploitation of all the forces in the cosmos. For this progress to continue and even be possible, what has already been achieved and discovered must be continually passed on and assimilated. In this process some things, perhaps inevitably, are forgotten and disappear. We no longer know, it is said, how to restore certain colors in the stained-glass windows of the cathedral at Chartres. In rebuilding our medieval cathedrals and town halls it is supposed to be difficult at times to find workers who know how to carve a window arch or capital out of stone.

Society itself is subject to constant change, and it is hard to be sure in what direction it is moving. Hegel speaks of progress in the consciousness of freedom.[1] Other prognoses predict the gradual metamorphosis of humanity into a "worldwide army of workers."[2] Sometimes change speeds up, as in an explosion. Violent revolution is a recurrent historical phenomenon, and its results are also, so it seems, for the most part ambivalent.

Within the same historical periods and, as it were, at right angles to the passage of time, national cultures exert mutual influence on one another in many different ways, creating hegemonies, dependencies, "alienations," and these then provoke the resistance of contrary movements. The role of the French language in Germany in the time of Frederick the Great is a famous example, but the Americanization of everyday German after World War II is basically a completely analogous process.

Again and again there are "renaissances," which attempt programmatically to win back something forgotten or suppressed and to restore it to esteem. Admittedly, the usual result of such "rebirths" is the unintentional creation of something completely new. What the Carolingian Renaissance of the time of Charlemagne thought of classical antiquity has a different appearance from the Hellenism of Winckelmann. Neither has especially much to do with the historical reality.

All these thoroughly different forms of historical events have, however, one thing in common. Without exception they aim at change, metamorphosis, a break with the past or its overthrow. They all "go with the times." Things must not remain the way they have been up to now. In the process of tradition, on the other hand—at least that is the way it looks at first glance—the situation is not only different, it is absolutely the opposite. Clearly we are not dealing with something new, evolution and metamorphosis. It is a question of preserving through all change the identity of something presupposed and preexisting, against the passage of time and in spite of it. All at once the slogans are fundamentally different. Instead of a "new way of looking at things" and "progress," we hear, "The Word they still shall let remain."[3] One passionately resists "another Gospel" (II Corinthians 11:4). Even Marxists talk of "the doctrine of the classics," which, although written more than a century ago, must be considered sacrosanct even today. In the sphere of this way of thinking we meet such concepts as deviation and orthodoxy, accommodation, *aggiornamento* and revisionism, reformation and demythologizing. All these concepts have a really defensible meaning only in the realm of tradition. Only there is preserving something originally given considered a vital necessity and a basic mission.

At this point, the question already arises: perhaps tradition, the concept and the thing itself, has a legitimate place only in the area of religious belief and "worldview." This question, I believe, goes to the core of the issue. It cannot be answered, however, with a simple Yes or No. Admittedly, it has been passionately debated over and over again in the humanities—in an especially constructive fashion in a uniquely dramatic debate at the start of the scientific era. This debate deserves to be recalled because of the significance of the participants, figures like Galileo, Descartes, and Pascal. Pascal played a leading role. He not only participated in the debate, he also attempted to explain its significance with a precisely formulated thesis about the realm in which tradition is valid.

II

This thesis is found in an essay composed by Pascal when he was twenty-four years old. Its title leads us to expect something completely different: "Fragment of a Preface to a Treatise on the Void."[4] (The treatise, by the way, was never written.) "The void," or more precisely nature's abhorrence of a void, *horror vacui*, is the real occasion and theme of this polemic.[5] *Horror vacui* was considered one of the fundamental forces of the physical world by the traditional natural philosophy of the age. "You know," Pascal writes in a letter from the year 1647, "how philosophers think about this subject: they hold as an axiom that nature abhors a vacuum."[6] Among contemporary philosophers who shared this opinion was, remarkably enough, Descartes. There is a touch of objective irony in the fact that in the same work that proclaims the principle of doubting everything traditional, he declares the traditional notion of *horror vacui* a compelling insight of reason.[7] Even Pascal, although he was at the time writing a treatise to refute this dogma of natural philosophy, says in a letter that he does not yet dare "to give up the axiom of *horror vacui*."[8] At any rate, he also formulates a general principle, which diverges from Descartes' in a characteristic way. While Descartes says that one should count as valid nothing that is not completely certain, Pascal finds it neither "right" nor "permitted" "simply to give up the maxims handed down from Antiquity, unless we are compelled to do so by indubitable and irrefutable proofs."[9]

Not even a man like Galileo Galilei could bring himself to ignore the prestige of tradition on the subject of *horror vacui*. Indeed, the popular opinion of the time seemed to be supported by experiment, the verifiable fact of the suction effect of pumps, siphons, and other hydraulic utensils. Probably, however, a *metaphysical* argument was more decisive: since "nothing" cannot exist, there can also not be a space in which there is absolutely "nothing."[10] Then, however, new and more precise experiments were made that threw doubt on this argument. About 1640, pump-builders from Florence confronted their famous fellow citizen Galileo, at that time fifty-seven years old, with the question: why could the suction effect of pumps draw water only up to a certain level, so that the *entire* "void" was not filled up. The only response Galileo could come up with was to modify slightly the principle of *horror vacui*. Then his disciple Torricelli conducted his famous experiment that solved the problem—at least that is what everybody believes—and refuted the old thesis. By filling a glass tube with mercury and then turning it upside down, he proved by an experiment the existence of the void that had been considered metaphysically impossible, what we still call in his honor the "Torricellian vacuum."

The polemics of this year and Pascal's letters reflect the unusual liveliness of the dispute that this experiment provoked. It is only comprehensible when you consider that a fundamental conception of the structure of the material world appeared to have been undermined, and a debate on method, which had been going on for centuries, had been settled.

As we said, it was Pascal who undertook to salvage from the debate an important and subtle distinction that was far removed from mere polemic, by clarifying the general problem of "tradition," the real if hidden subject of the discussion from the beginning.

Of course, Pascal did not disguise his disgust over the sterile methodology that "makes of every opinion of the Ancients an oracular response and sees holy secrets in its very obscurity."[11] At the same time he explains that he has no intention "of correcting one vice with another and showing absolutely no respect for the Ancients, just because some people have had too much respect."[12] Pascal's own constructive suggestion could be summarized, a little simplistically, as follows: obviously there are two different genres of human knowledge. One rests on experiment and rational argument, the other on tradition and authority. The prime example of the first genre is physics, where an appeal to authority and tradition is meaningless. The second genre is represented by theology.[13] Here only the transmitted word is valid. It makes no sense to talk about the Ancients in physics or in other sciences that are based on empiricism and rational argumentation. Strictly speaking, says Pascal, in comparison with men of bygone epochs it is contemporary men, the moderns, who are the "ancients." "The people we call the 'Ancients' are in reality in all things the beginners. They actually represent the youth of mankind. The 'antiquity' which we honor in them is really to be found in us, since we have added to their knowledge what the following centuries have learned."[14]

Pascal then surveys critically the intellectual situation of his own age. "Once we see this distinction clearly, we shall deplore the blindness of those who in physics want to treat as valid only tradition instead of reason and experiment; and we shall be shocked at the error of those who in theology replace the tradition of the scripture and the church fathers with the argumentation of reason. . . . Yet the confusion of this century is so great that in theology many new opinions receive a hearing which were unknown to the entire ancient world, while in physics new opinions, as few as they are, are supposed to be immediately considered false, if they contradict in the slightest traditional views."[15]

The fragment ends with a marvelous insight. "No matter what weight we assign to antiquity, truth must always be the prime consideration, however recently it may have been discovered. Truth is older than all opinions which people may cherish about her. People misunderstand her essence, when they believe that she first came into existence when she was first discovered."[16]

III

What exactly is meant by tradition? What is tradition?

One would think that these questions would be of basic interest to anyone engaged in philosophy. When, however, you try to get a preliminary orientation by turning to the standard German philosophical dictionaries,[17] you discover the surprising fact that they do not contain even an entry under the word. Curiously, they do discuss "Traditionalism," but not "Tradition." Maybe, you may say to yourself, the concept is viewed as reserved for theology, and so you consult theological reference works. There you will find information on the topic, but you will not find a great deal of help, since the concept is usually treated with a narrow concentration on the specifically theological meaning, as if there were not in everyday human language, as spoken and understood by ordinary people, a much more comprehensive but no less precise concept of tradition. Instead of discussing this topic there are articles on the problem of the theological controversy over "Scripture and Tradition." Sometimes "tradition" is understood as referring only to "the *oral* transmission of Christian truth."[18] Even Kittel's great *Theological Dictionary of the New Testament*, which is usually so outstandingly informative, offers on this topic only an unusually short and meager article, which cannot be compared with the rich documentation from the perspective of the history of religion, and even of philosophy, found in the articles it usually devotes to similar basic concepts—not to mention that the article on *paradosis* [the Greek word for "tradition"] appears under the main entry *didomi* [the Greek for "I give"].[19] Both from the point of view of content and of the difficulty of looking up the word, this makes about as much sense as putting the German word for tradition, *Überlieferung*, under the main entry *Lieferung*, or delivery.

Anyone who thinks of checking that tried-and-true classic of German scholarship, the Pauly-Wissowa *Real-Encyclopädie der classischen Altertumswissenschaft*, is in for a real surprise, unless he is an expert in Roman law. Under the main entry *traditio* there is indeed a clear and detailed article.[20] Without any reference to the lay usage of the term, it is completely devoted to the juridical concept in Roman law. "*Traditio* consists in a transfer of possession accompanied by an intention to transfer ownership."[21]

CHAPTER 2

THE BASIC ELEMENTS OF THE CONCEPT "TRADITION"

I

So we need to start at the beginning and try to name in order the individual elements out of which the concept of tradition is constructed as it exists in people's ordinary speech and thought.[1]

First of all it is immediately clear that when we characterize the concept of tradition as an activity, we are thinking of two partners. One person transmits, while the other receives something transmitted. This "something," which is occasionally also given the name "tradition," shall in the following pages be called what is handed down, *traditum*, or what is supposed to be handed down, *tradendum*. It can belong to any imaginable realm of human existence. The *traditum* might be knowledge or doctrine, but a legal maxim can be handed down, as can a song, a skill, a custom, a prayer, an institution, a power of attorney, a holiday, a norm of behavior. By this last I mean the way people address and greet one another, how people behave in church, how they receive a guest, and so forth. Our especial attention will be directed to the tradition of *truth*, where the *traditum* (or *tradendum*) is a teaching, a statement about reality, an interpretation of reality, a proverb. Of course, we have to acknowledge that a custom, a legal maxim and a holiday can contain a doctrine, explicitly or implicitly.

All these *tradita* have one thing in common: in every case we are dealing with something that can be received and handed down in a personal voluntary act. Maybe this sounds too obvious. There are, however, characterizations of the formal concept of "tradition" that appear to ignore this trait. For instance, tradition has been defined as "the aspect of life that continues to persist in different stages and generations," or as "the repetition of the same,"[2] whereby "the identity of what is"[3] is supposed to be preserved. This clearly means that what is to be handed down is that aspect of humanity which remains the same, maybe even man's "essence." Strictly speaking, this is not something that can be handed on as something to transmit, nor can it be received (or rejected) from someone who is transmitting it.

Next, there is still more to be said about the partners who have to deal with one another when tradition takes place. Whether it is a question of individuals or of generations, it must be clearly understood that they are not in a relationship of mutual influence. There is no give and take. Strictly speaking, there is no exchange of opinions. In fact, there is no exchange of any kind, not even a conversation, certainly not a dialogue. "But," someone could immediately object, "insofar as we are dealing with real life, do not fathers and sons have conversations in which both participate with equal right?" I would give the following answer: naturally, many things take place between the generations quite normally which are *not* tradition! When seen from the outside, the act of tradition itself may be difficult to distinguish from a discussion. In fact, they may be closely connected with one another and may turn into one anther. Tradition, however, is something fundamentally different from a discussion. It is quite normal for teaching and learning to take place between generations, and that activity may take up more time than any thing else they do together. Learning, however, is one thing. To receive something that has been handed down and to accept something transmitted as part of a tradition is quite another. We shall discuss this point in more detail later on. In concrete cases, of course, the difference, as I said, can be almost imperceptible.

Even in Plato's dialogues, which can count as the classic example of a discussion, of a "common inquiry," as Socrates is fond of saying,[4] the reader can easily miss the boundary at which suddenly the situation as a whole changes, where within a conversation—in which, despite all the clear differences of status, each of the friends, opponents, and disciples is participating with equal rights—unexpectedly an act of tradition takes place. When, for example, Socrates, at the end of the *Gorgias*, recounts the myth of Judgment after Death or when in the *Symposium* Diotima initiates Socrates into the mysteries of the ascent to Ultimate Beauty, something is going on that in its inner structure is absolutely different from the previous debates and discussions. Admittedly, Socrates does not remain completely mute in the presence of his partner Diotima, but he does not speak with her as a true equal. He asks and receives an answer. He is put in his place. Strictly speaking, his role is to listen and learn. This is not a conversation, but an act of tradition.

The partners who confront one another when tradition is taking place are not standing on the same level, although this does not mean that one has to be more intelligent than the other. Nevertheless, the transmitter is the speaker, and the recipient of what is to be handed down is at the same time the listener. Moreover, the two are not in a certain sense contemporaries of one another. They are not the same age, so to speak. Naturally, a conversation is taking place, which involves an exchange of ideas back and forth in time. The answer is always later than the question and the reply comes after the objection. Still, the intent is different in the two cases. The person who receives a *traditum* by listening receives it as a member or representative of the next generation. Even if by chance he were to be older in years than the transmitter, he is still the disciple [in German, *Jünger*] and heir to whom the tradition will be entrusted in the future. That is why Paul calls those who accept his message his "sons" (I Corinthians 4:14–15).

II

Is not the same situation, however, true for the relationship between a teacher and his pupils? Is tradition perhaps really the same thing as teaching? We have to grant that this usage does in fact exist. In both Greek and Latin we occasionally find the words for teaching and tradition used for one another. Plato says, "We say of the person who hands down information that he is teaching."[5] The same situation holds in Latin, "from Cicero and Caesar to modern papal encyclicals."[6]

Nevertheless, it is worthwhile, I believe, to be very precise about the meaning of the common usage of key terms, even if it causes the reader occasionally to lose his patience. In dealing with basic vocabulary, an apparently trivial inaccuracy can lead to a very significant obfuscation of entire conceptual areas. The number of possible examples of this situation is legion. Elucidation and understanding are simply impossible except on the basis of accepted linguistic usage. Even when someone proposes a definition that diverges from common usage and at first glance possesses a specious clarity, in his spontaneous thinking and speaking he remains unavoidably conditioned by common usage. The result is that he himself always ends up destroying the clear-cut precision of his own definition. On the other hand, everything that belongs to "actual linguistic usage" is incalculably large—for example, that a word cannot be used in a certain context. It is, therefore, really no simple matter to define explicitly the complete meaning of a word in common usage, although everybody, whether speaking or listening, means and understands without confusion.

All right, then, one more time. Is not tradition, insofar as we mean by that word the handing on of truth, basically the same as the communication of what is known by teaching from generation to generation? In brief, are not the words "tradition" and "teaching" synonyms?

At this point I would like to bring up the following consideration. The mere fact that it is possible to introduce a synonym for a certain word without changing at all the meaning of the sentence arouses the suspicion that we are using the words carelessly and not dealing with their true meanings. As long as I can replace the word "believe" with words like "think," "suppose," "assume" (as in the sentence, "I believe it is going to rain tomorrow"), I have not used the word "believe" in its strict and proper significance.[7] As soon as I use it that way, I find that there is no replacement, no synonym available.

Still, could the situation be slightly different in this case? No doubt any act of tradition (in the strict sense) can be called an act of teaching (speaking carelessly), insofar as by teaching nothing more is meant than bringing someone to know something that he did not know before. So in German you can say that someone who describes an event to me "instructs" [*unterrichtet*] me about what happened, although, as everyone knows, by "teaching" and "instructing" in the strict sense something quite different is meant from "reporting." "Tradition" and "teaching" are also, when the concepts are taken in their strict senses, two fundamentally different activities.

This matter becomes clear when we scrutinize the words for the act of tradition a little more closely. In the word "tradition" the Latin preposition *trans* is concealed. French expresses this clearly, since unlike Latin and German it has no verb directly formed from *tradition*. French describes the act of tradition by the verb *transmettre*. The preposition *trans*, however, when it is joined to a verb that expresses movement to a goal, contains, it seems, a clear reference to *three* different places. "Transporting," for example, means not only that something has been conveyed to somewhere or other, but also that something has been moved from a place where the transporter himself is not now located, to another, therefore to a third place. This means that we can talk about an act of tradition, in the strict sense, only when the person who is doing the handing on takes what he is sharing not from himself, but from "some other place."[8]

This same conceptual element comes out clearly in the verb with which English names the activity of tradition, *to hand down*. It would be worthwhile to devote a separate treatment to the word *down* here.

(Is it coming "downwards" in the time which is coming "upon" us?) I think, however, that we will learn more about this activity by pondering both directions that are assumed in common usage in English: *to hand down from* and *to hand down to* (*a person*). Again there are *three* places: someone, who stands in his own place, hands something "down" from somewhere else to another person. *To hand down* does not mean simply to give somebody something, to bring it, share it, or deliver it. It means rather to deliver something that has previously arrived in your hands, which was consigned to you; to share something that was handed over and handed down; to hand on something that you received—so that it can be received and handed on yet again.

"I received what I handed down to you"; "I handed down to you what I too received"; *quod a patribus acceperunt, hoc filiis tradiderunt*—"what they received from their fathers, this they handed down to their sons." The first two of these sentences are quotations from Paul,[9] while the last comes from the works of Augustine.[10] All three express more or less exactly the inner form of the act of tradition.

At the same time, they reveal clearly a crucial difference between the act of tradition and the act of teaching. When a scholar shares with his students what he has worked out for himself, his own discoveries, the results of his own research, clearly teaching in the strict sense is taking place, but not tradition.

III

From the hearer's point of view, learning corresponds to teaching. And here we need to repeat that the act by which a tradition is received is in its structure completely different from learning. It is at any rate clear that teaching has not taken place, if all that has happened is that something is pronounced *ex cathedra* and the listener goes away having been "lectured to," but without really learning anything. Similarly, the act of tradition is only completely realized when the last in line, the current last generation, really accepts and receives the *tradendum*. When this does not happen, for whatever reason, then tradition in the strict sense has simply not taken place. *One* reason for the non-acceptance can be the style with which the handed-down material is presented and offered. It is common for obstacles of this sort to be erected by the generation which is in charge. It is hard to commit a more hopeless act, for instance, than to respond to a young person who asks the question why and for what reason something handed down should continue to be valued with the words "it's just tradition." In such an evasion, at any rate, we see that the older generation no longer possesses a living image of what is handed down, and we are already dealing with what is called "bad preservation."

I was once the guest of a family in Calcutta who every day in their home had a Brahman perform the ritual of orthodox Hinduism in a room especially set aside for this purpose. When I asked about the meaning of some of the activities, the family's sons, who were university students, laughed in my face. And when I turned to the father with the same question, he shrugged his shoulders and said, "This has been done for a thousand years."[11] Shortly afterwards, when I left the house with one of the sons, he complained angrily that he had never heard any other explanation.

No one who wants to hand down a tradition successfully should talk about "tradition." He must take care that the content to be handed down, the "old truths," if they are really true, be kept really alive and present—for example and before anything else, by means of a living language; through creative rejuvenation and sloughing off the old skin like a snake, so to speak; through a continual confrontation with the immediate present and above all with the future, which in the human realm is the truly real. When you do this, you will see clearly what a demanding business the act of tradition is. There is a Hebrew proverb, "Teaching the old is harder than teaching the new."[12] It is especially clear here how little real tradition is something purely static, and how false it is to confuse the concept of tradition with inertia, never mind with stagnation. In truth, the activity of the living transmission of a *traditum* is a highly dynamic business.

IV

At this point we need to talk less about the act of tradition and more about that of reception. How does it happen that the last in line really participates in the tradition? Clearly it happens because someone accepts and receives what the person who hands down has offered him. But how are we to describe this act of accepting and receiving? At any rate, it is not just a case of taking in and holding onto knowledge. Just as the person who hands down tradition (and perhaps the one who is really teaching as well) is not interested in merely "providing information," so the attitude of the person who receives the *tradendum* is not that of someone who receives information. The practice of tradition does not at all have the form of "informing."[13]

A historian, for instance, can possess a very exact and extensive knowledge of the *tradita* and yet not accept them. Despite his knowledge he is standing outside the tradition. Perhaps his very knowledge is the obstacle to his accepting them. "Tradition vanishes, while perhaps all the documents are still there."[14] Karl Jaspers's statement expresses the extremely complicated problem of "historical research and tradition." Of course, accepting *tradita* presupposes knowing them. It is absolutely correct "that thanks to the historical and philological work of a century we stand in a more immediate and perhaps even richer participation in the teaching of the 'Ancients' (not only of the European world) than any earlier generation of recorded history."[15] Nevertheless, the act of accepting the *tradita* is not only fundamentally different from historical knowledge, it is actually threatened by historical knowledge.[16] So we can say in all seriousness that the modern "loss of tradition" and "tradition-less thinking" should be entered into the debit column of "historical consciousness."[17]

Suppose someone examines the results of historical research into problematic aspects of the details from which an ancient myth is formed, for example, the Judgment of the Dead. Sometimes the names of three judges are given, sometimes four. The name *Minos* points to Crete, but in Crete it appears to be a royal title, not a personal name. *Aeacus* comes from the totally different mythological tradition connected with the story of the founding of Troy, although the name also appears in the local legends of the island of Aegina. The word *Hades* is ambiguous; it may refer to a person or a place. Finally, *Acheron* is the name of a river in Epirus, whose course sometimes disappears under the earth's surface. And so forth and so on.

Anyone who reflects on all these individual facts may have some understandable difficulty in accepting simply as truth the "message" that is formulated in the myth of a Judgment after Death. He may be inclined rather to treat the whole thing as "just a story," like Callicles in the platonic dialogue *Gorgias*. Socrates, however, says, "I consider it the truth."[18] And he accepts this truth, he takes it seriously, *although* he knows and even says that no one could rationally prove that every detail is exactly the way the story tells it.[19] This means that the material from which the story is formed and the shell in which it is transmitted are not crucial. The crucial point is the message itself, which says in this case that there will be, on the other side of death, an event which will bring together the divine and human spheres, where the true results of our earthly existence will become manifest once and for all. In symbolic language this is called "the Judgment of the Dead." This message is the only thing that matters to Socrates. He considers it so valid that he orders his entire life in accordance with it.[20]

Precisely this is the nature of accepting a *traditum*, which is the question we are asking here. That is what the act looks like, in which the activity of tradition first reaches its goal and is consummated, by means of which alone someone "is part of a tradition" and participates in it. This is reception in the strictest meaning of the term, hearing something and really taking it seriously. I accept what someone else offers me and presents to me. I allow him to give it to me. This means that I do not take it for myself. I do not procure it for myself out of my own ability. On the other hand, I do not accept the *traditum* "because it is traditional," but because I am convinced that it is true and valid.

Whether this is correct, I cannot verify by means of experience or rational argument. Here I am in principle in the same situation as Socrates in the face of the traditional story of the Judgment after Death. Otherwise, I would not need to hear the message from someone else; I would already know it myself.

Taken all together, this means that accepting and receiving tradition has the structure of belief. It *is* belief, since belief means accepting something as true and valid not on the basis of my own insight, but by relying on someone else. *Who* in the process of tradition is this someone else? Is he the next-to-last person in line, or perhaps the first? It is still too early to discuss this problem.

Tradition is therefore, as we have said, different from teaching, and accepting something handed down is not the same thing as learning. But is it not the case, according to Aristotle's famous statement, that the learner too must believe?[21] This is true. But it is appropriate only in the first stage of learning. In the beginning of all learning we do not find critical checking, but an act of trust, which allows the student to accept without reservations what the teacher says.[22] Naturally, the same thing is true of the relationship of the infant child to his mother. Without this uncritical beginning we would never reach critical independence of judgment, which over time transforms what has been simply accepted into something that we know of ourselves. Only a person who has accomplished this critical transformation has really "learned," strictly speaking. Consequently, we could say with a certain justification that in this earliest phase the activity of learning is really similar to the activity of tradition—similar, but not the same. There is already at the earliest stage an important difference, which is that the teacher from the beginning already knows and recognizes of himself what he is teaching, whereas the person who hands down tradition can see through the *tradita* just as little as the recipient of tradition. No "older generation" knows any more about the Judgment after Death than the last in line, to whom this *traditum* is handed down.

V

It is an essential part of the concept of tradition that no experience and no deductive reasoning can assimilate and surpass what is handed down. And when such assimilation takes place, when something which had been believed becomes something verified and critically established, then in that same moment the process loses its character as tradition (if it ever really possessed it). It is therefore not correct to use the noun "tradition" to describe the process of learning that takes place collectively over generations and ages. In reality we are dealing with two completely different strands in the web of the historical process.

This is the place to discuss the suggestion of Alexander Rüstow, who wants to interpret tradition as "the inheritance of acquired characteristics and achievements."[23] For Rüstow this is precisely what distinguishes human beings from animals. In the famous experiments on animal psychology conducted by Wolfgang Köhler, the chimpanzee "Sultan" succeeded in the achievement of sticking two bamboo sticks together and using them to drag a banana into his cage. He accomplished this, however, for himself alone. It was absolutely impossible for him to transmit his accomplishment to his descendants. Rüstow wrote, "What animals truly lack, as opposed to human beings, is, precisely, not creative intelligence [*Geist*], but tradition—tradition as the possibility to disseminate what the mind has produced, to hand it down, and by preserving it to multiply and enrich it continuously from generation to generation."[24] This opinion may perhaps sound plausible at first, but it is full of inaccuracies. For example, it is precisely intelligence which allows human beings to hand down to successive generations not only what is innate, but also what has been acquired. The reason why animals are in no position to accomplish this is that they "lack" intelligence. Tradition is only conceivable as an act of intelligence. Handing down accomplishments is as little identical with tradition as "multiplying" and "preserving" are the same thing.

VI

We should discuss in this connection another element of the concept of tradition. It is precisely *the* element we use to distinguish tradition and cultural progress from one another. Cultural progress comes about by means of learning (in the strict sense). Something which originally was simply received is assimilated in turn by the younger generation in critical independence. They assimilate it, make it their own by their own experience and hard thinking, and then, after it has been corrected, augmented, and enriched, they hand it on. Then the next generation learns it all over again, i.e., at first it is accepted uncritically, but after that it is verified, corrected, supplemented, and enriched. To see more clearly what is unique about this process, we only need to compare it with the experience which sometimes happens to Westerners in so-called developing nations that are supplied with some item of cultural goods which is simply "accepted," but not really "learned." The cultural independence of a people is proven precisely by its capacity to penetrate critically what had recently entered its sphere and to advance through and beyond the previous situation of mere possession. This is the only way that the continual accumulation of items that were once handed down takes place, to which we give the name "progress."

Tradition, however, is fundamentally different. The concept of "progress" is completely out of place here. It certainly misses the essence of what is really going on. Thinking about individual originality and creative independence is inappropriate. We need to remember our previous characterization of tradition: the handing down of something received so that it can be received again and handed down again. We need to take this definition much more literally than is perhaps usually done. Let us remember Augustine's sentence, which was cited earlier, where, as I said, the formal structure of the act of tradition is precisely described: *quod a patribus acceperunt, hoc filiis tradiderunt.* In this sentence the word *hoc* is important. What is handed down is what has been received, and nothing else. This means that the last one in line receives from his "father" exactly the same thing as the first in line handed over to his "son." The *traditum* is something that in the accomplishment of the process of tradition precisely does *not* grow. As long as the intention that is devoted to the concept of tradition is allowed to maintain itself pure, explicitly no accumulation, enrichment, progress takes place. This intention aims rather at adding nothing to what has been received at the very beginning. Of course, it goes without saying that nothing of the original stock has been left out or forgotten.

People's customary thinking and speaking have never completely lost this aspect of the meaning of the concept of "tradition," as can be demonstrated. "*Sacred* tradition," especially, we can never picture as just a handing down of "achievements," a collection that men have acquired by their own efforts in the course of history. This can be shown more convincingly if we consider more closely some basic terms and ideas, which have always been part and parcel of talk about the concept of "tradition." In the first place we can name the idea of *preservation* and *maintaining purity*, which implies that an initial stock, whether it consists of a doctrine, a precedent, or an institution, is supposed to have been preserved and kept present and so to speak available without subtraction or addition, unadulterated and unmixed with anything foreign or inappropriate through the passage of time from the beginning.

The Hebrew word for appropriating what has been handed down means the same as "to repeat."[25] The Indians call this act of appropriation with the word "repeat after someone." Both designations make one thing clear: that even the slightest deviation will be avoided, that nothing will be left out and nothing added. The image behind the idea of *thesaurus*, the treasure chest, has a similar sense, although it is perhaps not so clearly expressed. The concept of *depositum*, a possession entrusted to someone, also belongs to this circle. One of the elements of its meaning implies that we are dealing with something that it is wrong for the person to whom the matter is entrusted to touch. More than that, he has been stripped of his power to use the object in his care.

What we have learned is our possession. What has been handed down to us we possess as a kind of loan.

The concept of *memory* is close to the concept of tradition and associated with it. They both have in common that something that has happened, or been experienced, or spoken once upon a time will be held present in the consciousness, will be "re-present-ed." This is often explicit. Tradition has been called "society's memory,"[26] "a culture's ontological memory,"[27] and *mnemosyne*, preservation through memory, has been described as that which does not allow "present and future to lose the fullness of being."[28] Remembering, however, means not only forgetting nothing, but adding nothing. It is a contradictory use of language if someone says he "remembers" something that exceeds the sum of what he actually experienced. Such a misrepresentation would be even worse than simply forgetting.

The vital necessity for tradition consists in the fact, as the old aphorism goes, that mankind has greater need of being reminded than of being instructed.[29] Human existence can come to grief not only because people neglect further learning, but also because people forget and lose something indispensable.

CHAPTER 3

TRADITION AND AUTHORITY

|

Accepting tradition has the basic structure of belief, i.e., relying on someone else. This amounts to saying that we cannot think of tradition without authority. During the entire Middle Ages "authority" was the name for tradition. *Auctoritas* and *ratio* were the technical terms for the two possible arguments used to establish proofs in a scholastic discussion, that is, by an appeal either to tradition or to reason. Goethe brought this connection to our attention and formulated it in his "Materials for the History of the Theory of Colors," where he links the concept of tradition to that of authoritative sanctioning: "While we are speaking of tradition, we are immediately compelled to talk at the same time of authority. If we are speaking precisely, every authority is a kind of tradition."[1] We find Karl Jaspers expressing the same thought clearly, although more objectively, and, as we shall show, not without reservations: "The crystallization of tradition into a fixed authority is unavoidable. It is . . . existentially necessary, since it [tradition] is the first form of certainty about existence for every awakening being."[2]

To questions about the reason for this identity or essential linking of tradition and authority, a first summary answer has to bring up the following considerations. Anyone who accepts a *traditum* as true and valid clearly does not himself possess direct access to what he is hearing from someone else. It seems to belong to the nature of the process of tradition that not only the one who is at the moment the last in line, but *all* the links are supported by and rely on someone of whom it is supposed that he is directly closer to the origin of the *traditum* and can testify to and vouch for its validity. Therefore, this closeness to the origin of the tradition provides the proof and basis for the authority of the one who is handing down tradition—the authority, of course, not of the penultimate in line, but of the first.

Up to this point we have spoken of the content of tradition with hints and examples. We have dealt with purely formal definitions, which are simply given by the structure of the process of tradition. It is already clear, however, what kind of opposition we have to reckon with from the beginning.

"Tradition stands in opposition to rationality." These are the words of Theodor W. Adorno in his in other respects rather imprecise "Theses on Tradition."[3] The sentence has a good Cartesian ring to it.[4] The medieval coordination of *auctoritas* and *ratio*, which we just mentioned, proves that, if we treat this thesis purely abstractly, we do not have to interpret it as an absolute denial of the validity of tradition. Nevertheless, the claim of "rationality," we must surmise, seems to mean that Adorno is here denying that existentially important relationships can exist that are exempt in principle from critical checking by human thought. The logical consequence of this view is that all tradition is banished at least to the realm of the preliminary and provisional. It rejects the idea of tradition in any absolute sense, as something that no effort of *ratio* can render obsolete and no progress of science can ever cancel or supersede. No one can accept this idea of tradition whose interpretation of human beings holds that it is contrary to the nature and dignity of their intelligence to treat information about reality as true and valid which cannot be "verified" either by experience or by rational arguments. There is no way to unite the assertion of the autonomy of reason and the recognition of tradition. If authority is really, as Karl Jaspers says, "the true enemy of philosophizing,"[5] then, despite all his nobly expressed insights that point in other directions, tradition must be repudiated as unacceptable to anyone who philosophizes, that is, to anyone who reflects critically and therefore is a truly intellectually alive human being.

Who exactly is it, however, on whom someone who accepts a *traditum* relies? How do we think concretely about the authority that guarantees the validity of what is handed down? In what historical form do we meet it?

II

One way to describe this authority since classical antiquity has been *palaioí, archaíoi, antiqui, maiores,* "the ancients," "the men of old." Who, we ask, is meant by this name? Who are the men of old, anyway? They are certainly not old people, *gerontes, senes,* the aged, those with experience or men "with snow-white hair." The youthful Pascal confused this meaning of the word with the true one. People have sometimes said that in using these names there is also a question of "respect for the elderly."[6] I do not believe that this is the case. It could be true that the founder of a line of tradition or, to speak more precisely, the first in the line, possessed at the same time the venerability of old age. It may even be true that it is impossible to imagine him without this venerability. Still, in the conceptual field of "the ancients" the decisive element is not the many years they have lived. And "respect for the elderly" is something fundamentally different from respect for the ancients. The essential element in this concept is closeness to the origin, the beginning, the early, the dawn, the start. The opposite of the ancients are later generations, those born after, who no longer possess a direct contact with the origin. They are therefore not the "young"—

whether or not in this last concept, as in Pascal's formulation, there is an emphasis on lack of experience or the still unused vital energy of the future.

Moreover, the name "ancients" is a thoroughly laudatory name. It does not mean the deceased, whose time is passed. Plato was convinced—and his conviction can lay claim to some weight in this matter—that the "wisdom of the ancients" is what is imperishably relevant, what "lives in everyone's words."[7] "The ancients know the truth. When we find it, then we do not need to concern ourselves with popular opinion."[8] This is the trait that distinguishes the "ancients" from the pioneers who open up new paths in scholarship. Of course, they too are respected, and we celebrate them when the hundredth anniversary of their birth or death appears on the calendar. They are, however, not really relevant or present any more. Later research has passed them by and corrected them in the meantime in many ways—by the very progress that they themselves have brought about. Their discoveries and judgments are today of only "historical" interest. On the other hand, we must say of the ancients that in the sphere of traditional knowledge they receive the same place as belongs to those who have made the latest discoveries in science.

Scholars have said that in Aristotle's opinion the "ancients" are the poets. He even calls them *pampalaioí*, the very ancient ones.[9] I am not convinced that Aristotle really held the "poetical" to be the decisive element. Plato, at any rate, distinguished between "divine" poets and the others, to whom he explicitly denied this quality.[10] Anyhow, he counted the former among those "who are wise in divine things." He did not include among them the latter. (I am thinking here of figures like Agathon.) Therefore, we must acknowledge that the "ancients" could of course be thought of as poets, but that in no way is it the poetical aspect that determines their belonging to the circle of the "ancients." The ancients are not identical with the great philosophers, and therefore not with the "noble minds" of whom Hegel says that, "having penetrated into the nature of things, of mankind and into the nature of God through the boldness of their reason, they have revealed to us their depths and gained for us by their work the treasure of the highest knowledge."[11] The status of the "ancients" is based not on their genius and the boldness of their thinking, but on the fact that in a completely unusual way they are the recipients of a completely unusual gift.

Plato refers to those he calls the "ancients" countless times in his dialogues, but they remain anonymous.[12] They are not figures who appear in person, like Crito and Phaedo. People speak of them, as we have said, as *palaioí* and *archaíoi*, but they do not have their own names. Often they are disguised even more deeply by expressions like *pálai légetai*, "it was said of old," "there is a wise saying of yore." That means that we shall turn back into the dark early morning of a *pálai*, the very first beginning, a prehistoric age, which we can neither imagine nor date. Nothing romantically vague is meant. Rather, we receive fairly precise information about what the "ancients" in truth were and in what the meaning of their "achievement" consists. This information is contained in a rather famous passage of the dialogue *Philebus*, which was clearly very influential.[13] The conversation has turned to the question of the relationship of the one and the many in the being of things. We do not have to discuss the basic problem and its significance. It is enough to see that it concerns the deepest structural form of reality. It is spoken of in the medieval doctrine of Being in direct connection with the theme of creation.[14] The important thing here is only that Socrates envisages the origin of this insight with unusual radicalness and speaks unexpectedly of the "ancients." "A gift from the gods was brought down by a certain (unknown) Prometheus in bright gleam of fire and the ancients (*palaioí*), better than we and dwelling closer to the gods, handed down (*parédosan*) this saying to us."[15] This is the definitive platonic formulation about the status and authority of the "ancients." Their dignity consists in the fact that they received from a divine source a message, a *phéme*, something spoken, and handed on what they had received in this way. This is the only reason why they are the "ancients."[16]

What Plato tells us here also clarifies another issue by giving us a still more precise answer to our initial question, one that confronts the foundation of tradition, that is: on whom does the last one in line really rely and depend? In whom does he really "believe," when he accepts what is transmitted as true and valid? What is it that in the last analysis vouches for tradition? The glance of the one who asks these questions turns naturally to the beginning of the line of tradition, to the first link in the chain. If it is really an essential part of the concept of tradition that everyone who transmits it, even the earliest in line, hands over something he received—that is, something that cannot be acquired or achieved by his own insight—from where and in what way does this first one receive the *tradendum*, what is to be handed down from this day forward? When Plato answers this question with a reference to the gods and the proclamation that comes to us from them, he is also saying that anyone who accepts and "believes" that tradition is relying, strictly speaking and fundamentally, not on the "ancients," but on the gods themselves—and, to be sure, also on the fact that what was given in this very first communication in the line of tradition has reached him safe and sound through the ages and the generations.

Plato, by the way, is not the only one to give us this information. The Roman conviction that the ancients stood close to the gods responds to him in almost the same words. Perhaps it was even inspired by him. (Cicero says, "Antiquity approaches most closely to the gods": *antiquitas proxime accedit ad deos*.)[17] The really exciting part of Plato's statement interests us not especially as interpreters of Plato or as students of the history of ideas. The exciting part is that Plato's statement in this matter is basically identical with the answer that Christian theology, for its part, gives to the same question. From this answer, ancient wisdom wins for those looking back at it a new significance that could not be surmised even by the ancient philosophers themselves. Just think about the individual elements of the platonic characterization: the "ancients" are closer to the divine sphere than the average man; they are "better" than we are, *kreíttones*, by which he probably means they possess a richer fullness of being, rather than that they are morally superior; most importantly, they are the first recipients of a proclamation which flows from a divine source and which they then hand on to human beings.

III

If you reflect on these basic elements of the concept of tradition one after the other, then there is hardly any question that there is at least a profound analogy between this description of the "ancients" and the definition by which Christian theology characterizes the "prophet," the "hagiographer," the charismatic called by God, someone who is "inspired" in the strict sense, the author of a sacred book. The common element, for which "analogy" is perhaps too weak a term, consists in the fact that both of them, the "ancients" and the "prophets," are thought of as the first recipients and transmitters of a *theios logos*, a divine speech, a word of God.[18]

At this point we need to consider an objection that is not completely unexpected. It will be raised by certain Christian theologians and rests only in part on a simple misunderstanding. Nobody should be surprised that a theology which makes the future and hope into its more or less exclusive theme will suspect that all talk about tradition and even more of the "ancients" is nothing but a kind of mythological and archaizing romanticism. Can the mere fact that there is talk of "in olden times" and "from of old" count as "evidence of truth"?[19] This question, at least, really rests on a misunderstanding that is relatively easy to clear up. Naturally, in the "wisdom of the ancients," even according to Plato's conception, the decisive element is not that it comes "from of old," but that it has its origin from a divine source. The ancients do not just stand at the beginning of time. They are the earliest in the chain of succession of tradition, the first recipients of tradition. And if a completely new revelation appears in history, "under Pontius Pilate," then its first recipients will have the quality that Plato attributes to the "ancients." It is therefore no objection to this conception that in fact Christianity has understood itself as something "new," as the beginning of a sequence of tradition that begins with a new divine proclamation.

It is more difficult to answer another problem, namely the assertion, intended as an objection, that for "traditional thinking" "revelation stands at the beginning."[20] This assertion is not completely unambiguous. It can mean either that a divine revelation took place "at the beginning"; or it can mean that it is an essential part of the concept of revelation that it must occur at the absolute beginning of things. Of course, no Christian can accept this second conception. Christ's revelation did not take place "in the beginning," but "in the fullness of time."[21] Plato and countless other intellects of the pre- and non-Christian world found themselves and find themselves in a situation that is fundamentally different. No other "divine speech" reached them except for the message embodied in and also to some extent disguised by the mythical narratives handed down "from the distant past," for instance, that tale of the Judgment of the Dead. This tale, however, really refers back to a divine revelation that took place "in the beginning," an "original revelation." I am convinced of this, in agreement with countless Christian teachers whose ranks reach from Justin Martyr and Augustine to John Henry Newman. I cannot answer with a simple "yes" the critical question, "Are the apostles to be equated with Plato's primeval ancients."[22] Still, I would insist that they are united by a decisive common element. It is not just that both are understood as the first recipients of a message that reached them from the divine sphere, and therefore they are the first links in the chain of tradition that began with them. There is also a more profound common element, which only the Christian can perceive in relation to the ultimate origin of the information attested to by both groups. That origin is one and the same: the divine logos that became man in Christ.

In any event, the concept of "revelation" comes into play as soon as one asks about the basis of the authority of tradition. We do not need to discuss this in detail right now, although it should also not be left exclusively to the debates of theologians. In the last analysis we are dealing not so much with an inter-theological theme as a pre-theological one. Insofar as theology is understood as the interpretation of revelation, theology can not even exist legitimately without presupposing the reality of revelation. On the other hand, if we take philosophy as what has been understood by the word from Plato and Aristotle all the way to Immanuel Kant and Karl Jaspers, then philosophical reflection on the world and reality can really not dispense with what is, I admit, a very difficult task. We need at least to discuss the question, whether, while considering all that we know critically about reality and human beings, it is meaningful to say and what meaning it could have to say that God has spoken specifically to human beings so that they could hear and understand.

Really, have we not left our theme completely behind at this point? We started out by limiting ourselves to asking about the basic elements of the concept "tradition." Now, I believe that we are still involved in treating that question. It is finally time to ask the following question: if someone who accepts a *traditum* as truth really and necessarily relies and depends on someone else, who then is this other person and what puts him in the position to vouch for the truth of the *traditum*? When we ask this, it is clear that we are being loyal to the intention we proclaimed in the beginning, to keep our attention focused on the handing down of doctrine and statements about the world, on what people may call the "tradition of wisdom." When we tried to investigate and name the guarantors of transmitted truth, our glance fell, not completely accidentally I admit, on Plato and his talk about the "ancients." A careful analysis of this conception unexpectedly brought the concept of "revelation" to the table. Finally, Socrates is relying on a divine speech when he accepts information transmitted "from the distant past" and makes it the plumb line of his conduct. He relies on the authority of revelation. All of a sudden we noticed that fundamental common element which links the platonic conception of the "wisdom of the ancients" with the Christian idea of a "sacred tradition" based on prophets and speakers called by God as the "original recipients of revelation."[23]

IV

All right, someone could now say, but on the other hand it is obvious that there are other traditions than the "*sacred*" tradition. Are there not clearly also secular and even very unholy traditions running through every area of our common human life? I agree, of course, although the facts of the case, as we shall soon see, are more complicated than is usually thought. One thing, however, has, I believe, become clear: there is only one way to think about a tradition of truth. It must be thought of as something definitive; that is, in principle, no human thinking can make it obsolete, insofar as people are convinced that what it transmits goes back ultimately to a divine speech, therefore to revelation strictly speaking. To this extent scholastic theology is right to make tradition and revelation almost identical[24] and to understand the concept of tradition as "the purely logical development of the idea of revelation itself."[25] Admittedly, it is wrong in another respect, which we shall speak of later on.

Of course, people who are of the opinion that ideas like "revelation" and "God's speech" just cannot exist, or, at any rate, do not in fact exist, must to be consistent not settle for holding every tradition of truth to be a temporary measure that will one day be surpassed and bypassed. They must believe that tradition cannot create a serious obligation for anyone. "Authority" can mean many things: belief, reliance, security, guarantee, but it also signifies a clear claim to be obeyed. A tradition can be absolutely authoritative, binding everybody fundamentally, only under the presupposition that it is guaranteed by divine authority, that is, because its origin is revelation.

To be sure, another presupposition is implied, one the modern consciousness does not usually acknowledge, namely, that everyman does *not* possess an immediate access to revelation. More than that, this everyman, even if above average, even if a genius, can participate in the divine proclamation only on the condition of being connected to its first recipients, the "ancients." Recognizing this contradicts, however, the claim of "free subjectivity" that has been called "the specifically modern form of religion."[26] If the individual consciousness has an "immediate access to the absolute," naturally it does not need the mediation of tradition. If, however, this mediation is understood as unavoidable and assented to, then this means that the authority of sacred tradition reaches as wide and as deep as the authority of the divine speech itself.

V

This authority, however, shows its real significance only when we speak of the *content* of tradition, a content we are obliged by such an absolute claim to accept.

What is the meaning of the details which have been announced to men in the sacred tradition as something that must be accepted? It goes without saying from the start that this special claim to obligation cannot be related to an unimportant content. One can simply not expect people as personal beings to be obliged to say without the possibility of critical verification, "this is the way it is and no other way," unless what has to be believed concerns the center of the world and the core of their own existence. It is precisely this which gives to the claim its full weight. What the "wisdom of the ancients" talks about, however, are in fact precisely subjects that concern the core and center.

Let us look at Plato once more. What does the "message transmitted from of old," of which we are told in his dialogues, have to say? It says that the world has arisen out of the ungrudging kindness of a creator;[27] that God holds the beginning, middle, and end of all things in his hands;[28] that spirit is Lord and rules over the whole of the world;[29] that mankind has lost its original perfection through guilt and punishment; that on the other side of death an absolutely just court awaits us all; that the soul is immortal—and so forth. Aristotle, too, who is so much soberer and more critical, says in frank agreement in the *Metaphysics*: "It has been handed down through the early ones and very ancient ones (*pampalaioi*) that the divine surrounds all nature in a circle."[30]

Anyone who turns from such discoveries to examine again the tradition of Christian doctrine soon (and also: again) meets with strongly expressed reservations, which are more or less as follows: surely you are not seriously pretending that "the content of the Greek tradition, 'handed down from of old,' [is] the same as the content of the Christian proclamation."[31] On one point I unhesitatingly grant the point the critical questioner is making: neither Plato nor any other pre- or non-Christian mind could have had the slightest inkling of God's incarnation or Christ's passion, death, and resurrection. And yet a great Christian theologian, Thomas Aquinas, was not afraid to think and say that, even outside the explicit revelation of Christ, it was possible for someone to believe that God, in a manner pleasing to Him, was going to become "the liberator of mankind"—which is as much as to say, to believe in Christ *fide implicita*.[32]

So it seems to me that it is not totally farfetched to believe that, despite all the profound uniqueness and "newness" of the revelation of Christ, the "sacred tradition" of which Plato, for instance, speaks could share a common content with the Christian proclamation. In both cases it is said that God himself vouches for the meaning of the world and human salvation. If, however, this naturally very summary formulation names accurately their common content, then we are not only justified, but we are compelled to think of the revelation and promise that has been granted to us in Christ as linked to the very earliest beginnings of human history and with what pre- and non-Christian humanity "from of old" has believed as sacred truth and preserved through the millennia. After all, the motto *pálai légetai*, which refers to God's speech resounding though human history "since forever," stands not only in the platonic dialogues, but also in the first verse of the *Epistle to the Hebrews* in the New Testament.

If, therefore, the *tradita* that are to be accepted and handed on, so that they will be accepted again, are really as we have described them, then the question about the basis of the obligation to accept them and hand them on can be answered more adequately. At any rate, the theoretical possibility of such an answer exists. In reality, of course, both the question and the answer are usually formulated in a very concrete historical situation—you might almost say, in a definite phase of the debate between fathers and sons. And both question and answer soon move far away from their theoretically possible arguments.

It is completely normal and comprehensible for each new generation to call into question the obligation towards tradition. There is really nothing praiseworthy in the mere fact that something which has been thought, said, or done "since forever" will continue to be thought, said, and done. The praise due the act of tradition only makes sense when what is preserved and will continue to be preserved through the generations is *what is truly worth preserving.* That is the point of young people's doubting question. Why is it, they ask, that a duty has been violated, if we simply let what had been handed down rest on its laurels, so that we can say, think, and do something totally different? We can only hope that someone hears this radical question and gives an existentially believable and equally radical answer, "the" answer that goes to the heart of things: that among the many things that are more or less worth preserving and may have been accumulated as "tradition," there is in the last analysis only *one* traditional good that it is absolutely necessary to preserve unchanged, namely the gift that is received and handed on in the *sacred* tradition. I say "necessary" because this tradition comes from a divine source; because each generation needs it for a truly human existence; because no people and no brilliant individual can replace it on their own or even add anything valid to it.

CHAPTER 4

IS THERE ONLY *SACRED* TRADITION?

I

It is now time to discuss the objection, which has been waiting for a hearing, that after all there is more to tradition than *sacred* tradition. As we have already said, the objection is absolutely correct. Whenever and wherever norms of behavior, customs, conceptions, opinions, and institutions are handed on through successive generations in order to be handed on again, if not necessarily as authoritative, yet without explicitly critical questioning, tradition is taking place there. It would be an endless task to try to survey the different forms of such thoroughly "secular" traditions in an orderly fashion.

The existence of these traditions is of absolutely vital significance for the communal life of mankind. First of all, they serve an indispensable function of liberating and unburdening the individual conscience and social interactions. Our common life can run along with less friction, and human energies can be turned without let or hindrance to their real goals, when it is taken for granted on the basis of unquestioned tradition that, for example, people say hello to one another on the street; that at a party you introduce yourself to someone you do not know; that you say thank you when someone helps you; that you say excuse me or pardon me; that everybody uses the usual forms of address; that you do not talk about private and personal issues with just anybody; and so on and so forth. "The reality of manners and morals . . . is and remains to a great extent valid because of convention and tradition. They are freely accepted, but are not in any sense created out of free insight or based on the validity of free insight."[1] It would be an unendurable burden on our common life if every decision about everything that has to be done were decided from case to case on the basis of critical reflection.

The *Wandervogel* [Bird of Passage] generation after the First World War called into question, along with many other "bourgeois" customs, the use of the polite form of address *Sie*.[2] Of courrse, they could adduce many historical and critical objections: why are we talking to one another using the third-person plural, as though we were at the Spanish court? But what a disproportionate expense and loss of efficiency it took to replace *Sie* with a new form (*Ihr*) [the familiar plural]. When I was growing up, nobody said, when leaving, *Auf Wiedersehen*. This expression, which has since become completely traditional and is recognized throughout the world as "typically German," first appeared in the years 1914–15 as the result of "national" propaganda to replace the formerly uncontroversial French *Adieu*. Would it have been worth the effort to organize opposition to the change? Maybe someday an expert in cognitive psychology will discover that it will be better to use different colors than green and red in traffic lights. Is that a reason to change the status quo?

In his general discussion of human legislation, Thomas Aquinas once asked the question whether a law should always be changed as soon as a better rule was possible.[3] His answer begins with the distinction between an argument based on reason (*ratio*), on the one hand, and custom and usage (*consuetudo*), on the other. Since, however (he continues), the power of laws to compel assent is strongly determined by *consuetudo*, the very fact of change in itself represents injury to the common good, and it is for the sake of the common good that laws are made in the first place. Therefore, in a particular case it could be thoroughly reasonable to allow a human tradition to continue in force for the sake of preserving continuity, even though the concrete *traditum* may be in itself problematic. At any rate, it is clear from his discussion that "preserving continuity" and "preserving a *traditum*" are not the same. In America, during a newspaper interview, I was once asked directly my opinion about what Thomas Aquinas would have said about the Negro problem—"integration or segregation?" I answered that he would certainly have favored integration, but would probably have added the advice: pursue it without yielding, but slowly, one step at a time! Many prudent Americans from both North and South told me that they agreed.[4]

II

We need to talk a little bit more about "secular" traditions. It should be clear by now that their authority is of a different sort from that of sacred tradition. Possibly a custom that was intended to make human life easier becomes positively burdensome when social circumstances change—so much so that it becomes almost a duty to do away with it. What would happen, for example, if on a walk through a crowded city street you had to take off your hat to every person you recognized? Obviously, there was never an obligation in the strict sense to do so, not even fifty years ago. Nevertheless, in a concrete case simply waving your hand could be interpreted, perhaps rightly, as "impudence." In such matters there are no general standards of judgment. Perhaps the social critic's desire to change, viewed purely abstractly, is right as often as is simple respect for what was once customary.

The graduating class of my old high school still, "according to old usage," makes a solemn procession through the town in a horse-drawn carriage.[5] It is getting hard these days to find a horse and carriage for this. Someday it will be impossible—and this tradition will therefore disappear. Should we say, "What a shame?"

In my grandparents' day, it was a settled custom in peasant households that the father had to slice the bread for suppertime. If he was beginning to cut a new loaf, he made the sign of the cross over it with the knife. It was done, as I saw many times as a child, almost casually, even furtively, but it was never omitted. Things have changed since then. We no longer bake those enormous loaves of black bread, which really needed a grown man to master them. Now we have machines to slice the bread, and most of the time the bread comes from the store or factory already sliced. In a word, this beautiful tradition too has passed away. It does not take much imagination to see how many themes are present here for a truly pessimistic cultural critique ("machines replacing humans," "urbanization," "the collapse of the family," and so forth).

Nevertheless, we can ask whether this kind of change is simply deplorable. Is it legitimate to speak in a more or less precise sense of a "loss of tradition" here? The answer to this question is made more complicated by the fact that here the purely technical process was clearly linked with elements of the sacred tradition. It seems to me that we could really talk about a "loss of tradition" and a "break with tradition" if the change affected the family's order, and most of all what was meant by the holy sign of the cross; that is, such language is appropriate when that which is lost stands in more or less direct connection with the *traditum*, which alone must be unconditionally preserved. It is common for the essence of what must be preserved to become overgrown by and entangled with the concrete forms of historical life, and a change in the outer may very well threaten the pure preservation of the essence, so that anyone who carelessly discards or makes light of the "outer" traditions commits a dangerous act. A student of ethnology once told me that in a group that was driven out of its homeland, religious commitment might possibly grow looser to the same degree that the group moves away from baking its rolls in a certain way. Of course, the question remains open what is the cause here and what the effect, and whether we are not dealing with an extremely complex total process.

We still have to confront the question of the unique character of sacred tradition and whether it and it alone can really be called "tradition." Two things have grown clearer in our discussion, I believe. The *first* is this: only in a sacred tradition that goes back to a divine speech does the first in line hand over something actually received, that is, something not confirmed by his own insight. This is, considered purely formally, the purest imaginable form of tradition. *Second*, again because of the divine origin of the *traditum*, the sacred tradition can be matched by no other form of tradition in respect to its authoritative character and power to create an obligation. It has even been said, "a special revelation through God's Word" establishes a "traditional connection" that is so strong that there is an analogy with it "in no other field."[6]

A certain authority is of course possessed by the forms of human interaction that are in normal cases simply accepted by each succeeding generation, so that disregard for things that "one" usually does can *in concreto* be an act of out-and-out injustice. There is also a kind of obligation in the collective process of learning, which keeps cultural progress going. Alexander Rüstow has spoken about respect, trust, and reverence before authority and has described it as the basis for "the way culture descends socially from generation to generation; and whoever undermines these feelings, is shaking the ultimate foundation of human culture."[7] The theologian will perhaps understand the biblical imperative to "subdue the earth" (Genesis 1:28) in the same way as a binding injunction.

Nevertheless, one hesitates to speak of an obligation that binds individual people to work together for the progress of civilization. In the area of the purely cultural there is hardly a basis for a binding obligation by which a person would be duty-bound to preserve and hand on something that came to us created by humans, whether this is the materialist "doctrine of the classics," Marx, Engels, Lenin, and Mao, or any behavior that has become "institutionalized." There is a "tradition" of celebrating your mother's birthday, or Mardi Gras, or Schützenfest [Marksmen's Fair], or May Day, or "German Unity Day," but any of these can be confidently ignored, if the time is not convenient. One may even consider whether a public holiday, which has been established in a certain situation, may not be abolished. Not to celebrate *Easter*, however, even if it falls in periods that are far from "festive," stands on a different footing. It is a completely different affair. It involves violating an incomparably more serious duty. It is an obligation we find only within *sacred* tradition. If sons really did stop celebrating the religious holidays celebrated by their fathers, or if the *tradita* of the sacred tradition were no longer accepted and handed down, here alone we must talk about a "loss of tradition," of a "a complete lack of tradition" and a "break with tradition."

Tradition is by no means a confused mass of historically transmitted accidents, wherein everything that has been created and preserved, as long as it possess a certain antiquity, is equally valid (or equally invalid, as the case may be). A proper distinction and ordering is only possible if the unique status of sacred tradition is recognized and accepted. It is TRADITION within tradition.[8] Yves Congar has distinguished between "The tradition" (singular) and the plural "traditions."[9] This distinction, which corresponds exactly to the real state of affairs, allows unexpected possibilities of understanding to develop, both in the historical past and in the present. Someone, for example, who is accustomed to regard the Middle Ages all too summarily as an age completely under the dead hand of tradition, now has the opportunity of grasping why the great teachers of the thirteenth century called the argument from tradition, *locus ab auctoritate*, the weakest of all arguments.[10] By this they meant explicitly *not* the appeal to "the tradition" but one to "the tradition*s*." The explicit respect for the unimpeachable character of the sacred tradition presupposes the possibility of relativizing other traditions and in fact makes it possible and reasonable. The connection, which may be at first glance surprising, recurs over and over again and is not about to lose its relevance in our day.

III

The more decisively the energies of the conservative instinct, the will to preserve, are directed at what is definitely worth preserving, the more change in external matters that can be put up with and even encouraged without fear of a "break." Genuine consciousness of tradition makes one positively free and independent in the face of conservatisms, which worry obsessively about the cultivation of the "traditions." Certainly, a "cultivation of tradition" that attaches itself to a historically accidental external image of what has been handed down becomes a positive hindrance to a real transmission of what is truly worth conserving, which perhaps can occur only under changed historical forms. It is possible to imagine a real transmission of what is in the last analysis worth handing down, which a dogmatic conservatism could not even recognize.

On the other hand, the fact that Tradition (singular) naturally takes the form of the plural traditions and so becomes deformed should not be misinterpreted as a call to indiscriminate experimentation and innovation in the social and cultural field. What is needed here is a lucky and perhaps very rare linking of prudence and courage. For this mixture there is no once-and-for-all recipe. Negatively we can say with certainty that it will never succeed—except on the basis of a hearty assent to the divine gift that is intended for us in the sacred tradition.

If, however, this gift—whether information, a wise saying, or a sacrament—is taken up into the practice of daily life, it soon becomes clear that it cannot be kept under lock and key (so to speak). The obligation to preserve it pure, which remains in any case strictly demanded, is something completely different from keeping a gem locked up in a treasure chest. The fact that a tradition is "sacred" does not mean that what is handed down in it is something "specifically religious" and therefore belongs to a definite, clearly delimited field, but is otherwise unimportant.

The platonic Socrates unceremoniously introduces the *traditum* of the Judgment after Death into a highly relevant philosophical and political debate that he is carrying on with a practitioner of power politics, and he is absolutely right to do so.[11] His interlocutor, Callicles, will not let himself be convinced that *doing* injustice is worse than *suffering* injustice, and that the obligation to justice is unconditional. And as the rational part of the discussion finishes in a dead end, Socrates presents what is objectively his strongest argument—well aware, of course, that he is speaking to deaf ears now and in the future. This argument is the story of the Judgment of the Dead, which has been handed down "from the distant past." The truth of this story, if it is only accepted and reflected on, aims at changing completely the practical life of men in the historical *polis*. Not a word is devoted to the objection that the story is a bizarre esoteric secret doctrine, which is of no relevance to the "practical man" and especially not to the "politician." You can look it up in the *Gorgias* and see for yourself how vividly Socrates brings this myth to life.[12]

In the same way, for instance, it makes an enormous difference for practical conduct in the world whether or not one accepts the *traditum* of the created character of the world and mankind. Only someone who accepts it, who understands mankind essentially as something designed, can stand up against Jean-Paul Sartre's thesis, which is equally derived from a dogma, has very serious consequences, and is by no means purely abstract. Since there is for Sartre no human nature and human beings have no preestablished purpose or meaning, they possess no way to orient their lives toward any kind of "sign" or any obligation or commitment, however formed.

Take a sentence like this one out of the biblical report of the creation: "God formed man out of the clay of the field and breathed into him the breath of life" [Genesis 2:7]. What this sentence truly means must be continually reformulated. Today, for instance, we need to reflect further on everything that we know critically about what paleontology and evolutionary theory tell us about how mankind arose. Otherwise, the contents of the sacred tradition cannot maintain their relevance to the present day. Anyone who does not undertake this new formulation frustrates and neglects what is by definition the goal of all tradition: mankind's real sharing in the *tradendum*.

IV

Grappling with this unending task is—in the case of the sacred tradition—the business of theology. Rather, this is exactly what theology *is*: the translation, which has to be revised over and over again under continually changing circumstances, of the "original texts" of the *tradita* into a form that can be understood by the present historical moment. Actually accepting the challenge implicit in that task seems to be something distinctively "Western." Maybe we must also say that we are dealing with a specifically *Christian* phenomenon. At any rate there is apparently no theology in this sense in the non-Christian world.

In Indian universities, for instance, I have many times had the experience, while talking with professors of the Sanskrit Department (which corresponds more or less with our Theological Faculty), that they see neither the possibility nor the necessity of confronting in any way the religious tradition of Hinduism with the natural sciences taught in the same universities. The inevitable consequence is, on the one hand, the sterility of the body of tradition, which is only continuously repeated and recited in cult. On the other hand, the younger generation is left in the lurch, since in this way they lose the connection to their own spiritual origin. The only ones who undertake the perhaps hopeless attempt to make available and hold present the truth hidden in the Indian doctrine of the gods through interpretation and "translation" are Christian missionaries from Europe.[13]

We can see here, if anywhere (to repeat myself), how exciting and dynamic the act of tradition is. People simply miss the true situation when they oppose "tradition," as what stays the same, to "history," as the essence of change. For one thing, the preservation of the *tradita*, even "bad" preservation, is one process within the total process "history," just as much as the rise and fall of empires or the increasing exploitation of the forces of nature. In addition, the effective presence of the *tradita* can only be achieved as the result of an eminently historical effect—"historical" now understood in the stricter sense of immediate relevance.

The formula of "tradition and progress," which has become a popular mantra, is hardly worth discussing. At best it has a propagandistic character and implies that someone is "going with the times" without, however, abandoning something "tried and true." First of all, just because something is "tried and true" does not necessarily mean that it is a *traditum*, or even anything really worth preserving. Worse, this formula all too easily strangles in the cradle the insight that there is hardly anything that would be more helpful for progress in the future than to take a divine gift shared with mankind long ago and make it come alive to human thought by reminding us of its importance through representation and interpretation. This very active reminding is not directed, as a foolish and fashionable formulation has it, to "what used to be," but to what is always valid and relevant for every age and which is continually threatened by forgetfulness and corruption.

In relation to this act of interpreting the *tradita*, which must be undertaken anew in every age, there can certainly be progress. There can, however, scarcely be serious doubt that a more profound understanding and interpretation of the *tradita* does not simply and so to speak of itself appear in step with the progressive accumulation of historical facts. Rather, it depends on the openness and powers of penetration of the mind of a person. In the case of interpreting revelation—that is, theology—are we "more advanced" than Jerome, Augustine, or Thomas Aquinas purely because knowledge has naturally increased and accumulated over the centuries? The question, I suppose, makes about as much sense as asking whether Goethe was "more advanced" than Homer or Kant "more advanced" than Plato. It is not that there is no progress in this field, but when advances are made, it is not on the basis of the simple passage of time.

In the case of the sacred tradition, the goal is always to represent *identically* what was originally shared with mankind from a divine source. As an *epigonus*, I am really interested in this and this alone, not in reformulations and new interpretations as such. I am only interested in using the interpretation that represents the tradition as a means to help me gain access to exactly the same thing that the first recipient of the message had access to: salvation, knowledge, wisdom.

In this connection, Plato used the word "save." The mythical story of the Judgment of the Dead and reward or punishment in the afterlife was in marvelous fashion "saved." He then astoundingly adds the wish that it "can save us too, if we believe it."[14] If the identity of this treasure, which has to be salvaged anew in each age, were to be lost, that would mean that the most important thing was lost, namely what was really meant by the revelation. The increasing differentiation of the categories used in interpretation and the ever more precise understanding of what was truly meant is, naturally, a fascinating theme for historical reflection and should not be called "the evolution of dogma."[15] Insofar as I am a believer, however, i.e., someone who as the last in the series desires the "proclamation which has reached us from the past" itself, this theme is of no interest to me. My primary interest is in the divine speech, not in theology.[16]

A theology, on the other hand, which does not concern itself before anything else with the task of preserving through the ages the divine revelation that has been proclaimed to mankind alive and identical, which perhaps instead of this is occupied with reflecting and interpreting in a relevant way the religious impulse of the age (or what are taken for religious impulses)—if possible using biblical concepts and terminology—such a theology does not deserve the name "theology."

CHAPTER 5

WHERE IS SACRED TRADITION HISTORICALLY FOUND?

I

If we ask where in the historical world "sacred tradition" is actually found, we are first and foremost referred to Christian theology, or rather to its object, the tradition drawn from Christ's revelation. This question is meant here not so much as an introduction to a principled discussion of the "only true religion," but rather as an inquiry that can be empirically answered. Where in the world does anybody as a matter of fact make the claim to transmit information that is divinely vouched for and concerns the whole of reality and the center of human existence? It is worth considering that this information, insofar as someone wants to possess it and participate in it, is to be received as something that must be simply accepted. The immediate answer to this inquiry is clear: the tradition of Christian doctrine makes precisely this claim. Christianity understands itself in fact on the basis of the commission to be obliged to preserve from both forgetfulness and contamination with foreign elements a divine proclamation that was spoken once inside of history and to hand it down as sacred tradition in a clearly joined "succession."

In every sacred tradition the real *agens* is the concern to prevent the loss or corruption of what was entrusted to mankind once upon a time "in the days of old" through divine revelation. In addition, it must be handed down to the coming generations identically, as itself. One needs only to consider this fact for a moment to see how silly it is to measure the church by the demands of "progressivism." This demand belongs nowadays to the "confusion of the century," about which Pascal too speaks. It consists in not making necessary distinctions, in measuring an institution founded explicitly for preservation with the same standard of judgment as the institutions of scientific research and the technological conquest of the natural world. It belongs, in fact, to the nature of these latter institutions for the sake of always progressing research into physical reality that they must surpass, correct, and even sacrifice what is already known. Of course, the *tradita* too have an unceasing need for interpretation and reformulation in order really to reach each new generation. (We have already talked about this at some length.) This process, however, by its nature has the character of "translation," and we can only speak about translation, as everybody knows, as long as the identity of the original text exists and remains preserved. Naturally, such a claim to identity cannot be proven believable and maintained for a long period unless the *tradita* are treated as a divinely vouched-for proclamation and really are so. They have to be more than and different from Marxism's "doctrine of the classics."

II

And yet it would be an inappropriate narrowing of the true state of affairs to see "sacred tradition" realized only in the realm of biblical and Christian doctrine. It is narrow-minded to define tradition, taken as process and act, as nothing more than "the ecclesiastical proclamation of belief, which began with the Apostles . . . and was continued by their successors with the same authority."[1] Such a limitation of the term is even theologically questionable. Can one dispute so simply the claim of the mythical tradition in the pre- and non-Christian realm to preserve through the ages knowledge which equally comes down from a divine source—especially insofar as we are convinced that there existed, long before the "Apostles," something like an "original revelation"? This last concept, which we have mentioned before, does not have an especially high standing in the current discussion, if indeed it is mentioned at all.[2] It has been at home in Christian theology, however, since the earliest times and it will always recur to memory as something indispensable. The concept of "original revelation" betokens that at the beginning of history an event took place of a divine speech directed especially to "the" man, that is to *all* men, and that what was shared at that time has entered into the sacred tradition of all peoples—in their myths, that is—and is preserved and present there, more or less recognizably. Augustine, in his late work the *Retractationes*, formulated this thought—admittedly in a way that is all too easy to misunderstand and has in fact often been misunderstood: "The very thing which is now called the 'Christian religion' existed among the ancients. Indeed it has never been absent since the beginning of the human race, until Christ appeared in the flesh. That was when the true religion, which already existed, began to be called the 'Christian religion.'"[3]

Anyone who considers the concept of "original revelation" to be valid, with whatever reservations he may have, and is at the same time convinced that "all that and only that which is the object of revelation is also the object of tradition,"[4] will find it hard to reject the conclusion of recognizing the original tradition that is linked with the original revelation as a fundamental form of "sacred tradition."

Drawing this conclusion, however, would have very interesting consequences! For example, one would have already accepted that such an original sacred tradition, derived from the same *logos* which became man in Christ, not only occurred "once upon a time in the past" in the *pre*-Christian era, but that it still exists in some sense in the "pagan" peoples and cultures today. At this point, we need to talk somewhat more precisely about the words "in some sense."

First of all, I would not like to associate myself with a "gnostic" or romanticizing interpretation of myths, such as is found in the works of Leopold Ziegler.[5] It seems to me simply *not* possible to ascribe a quasi-absolute value to stories that take place between the divine and human sphere—that is, to myths—as they are actually found in the realms of European classical antiquity, the high cultures of the East, and "primitive" peoples. What I venture to assert is much less than that, namely the following: in the stock of the "mythical tradition," which is polymorphous and difficult to reduce to a unity, along with many kinds of heterogeneous elements there exist also *tradita* in the strict sense. This too is a "place" in which "sacred" tradition in the full significance of the word "sacred" really occurs. To put it another way, there is something present which is not yet correctly named if one speaks, like Hegel, of early images created by "imagination at play,"[6] or, as is common in the learned literature on Plato, of poetical simile speech created out of the "symbolic power of myth" by the consciousness of a genius.[7] The essence of the phenomenon is missed if "myth" is defined as "a religious narrative, which is clearly understood to have been formed by men and which can therefore always be further recreated by them in new forms."[8] This description is clearly refuted by the attitude of the platonic Socrates before the myths he tells and, in addition, by Plato's own words, according to which "it is meet and right to believe the old and sacred sayings, which tell us that the soul is immortal and will come before the judge."[9] Let us formulate this in a positive form. In the mythical tradition there is something which can only be appropriately grasped and characterized when it is understood as the more or less clear echo of a speech of God that took place in the beginning—that is, as a revelation.

The word "echo" should make clear that the *tradita* in the mythical tradition are usually not preserved in a pure form. Their true form has not remained immediately recognizable. It is hidden beneath a thicket of fanciful additions. The genuine has been deformed and mangled, and the Christian may be right to think (also) of demonic distortion. A good parallel can be found in the platonic *Republic*, where the present state of the soul is compared with the marble statue of the god of the sea, with its limbs broken to pieces and crusted over with mussels, seaweed, and gravel, so that it looks more like a monster than what it really is.[10] Plato seems to have surmised that even the great mythical narratives with which he ends some of his dialogues are only broken shards, fragments of a tradition which can no longer be grasped as a whole—no longer or not yet. A late dialogue speaks of this situation explicitly.[11] Some elements of the wonderful old stories have been completely obliterated in the course of the ages, others have been scattered far and wide, and individual parts have been separated from their place in the whole. No one has yet been able to identify the cause of all this. One scholar has even suggested that this is the awe-inspiring achievement of Plato himself: to purify the scattered fragments of accretions and reassemble them into the "ancient interpretation of the world" found in the true "great myth."[12] It is precisely this task of separating the true from the false inside the material that has actually survived, however, which surpasses completely Plato's capacity and that of pre-Christian thought as a whole. We could even say that this is the tragedy of the platonic Socrates, that, on the one hand, he stands on the solid foundation of a sacred tradition against the Sophists' conscious denial of tradition, and so accomplishes his mission *without*, on the other hand, being able to formulate precisely the content of the tradition. Since, however, he refuses to treat the myths as "just stories"; since, on the contrary, he unflinchingly accepts and honors what is meant by them as truth, the *tradita* of the divine guarantee of human salvation are for him so unforgettably present that he can dare to base his existence on them.

You might ask, *what is the reason* that Socrates "allows himself to be told" the mythical information that comes from the gods by the "ancients," who remain for him unavoidably nameless. Why does he believe in them? We might give the following tentative answer. It has always been treated as belonging to the nature of the case that whoever believes in another person by that act wants and realizes "spiritual union"[13] and communion with him. "We believe because we love."[14] This communion with the witness and surety is therefore the presupposition on the basis of which and by means of which someone "believes"—whether we speak of Socrates or ourselves. The believer is always a member of such a corporate body, which is present invisibly in the history of mankind and really does have an effect, although admittedly one hard to grasp empirically. Perhaps the most appropriate name for it is *Corpus Mysticum*. As everybody knows, this is the expression Christianity uses to describe itself. Even Karl Jaspers, however, cannot dispense with it in order to name, with unavoidable vagueness, that "kingdom of minds" to which the philosophizing person gives his allegiance in faith, but which is "not objective anywhere."[15] Admittedly, that sounds like unrestrained "speculation." And it would be all too flimsy if it could not appeal to the assumption of an original revelation. In fact, however, it has its eye on exactly that *Corpus Mysticum* which encompasses ages and cultures and which is founded on the common possession of a truth guaranteed by God. And the sacred tradition, "a function of the community founded by revelation,"[16] justifiably appears to be what Viacheslav Ivanov says it is: the only power that can again "unite us with the origin, and with the word that 'was in the beginning.'"[17]

As decisively as the mythical tradition needs the purification, refinement, and interpretation made possible by means of the power of the *logos* that finally and definitely appeared among mankind in order to reach its own truth, just so does it ill suit Christendom to ignore the dignity of the *tradita* present in the mythical tradition—however difficult it may be to recognize the original speech in the echo. In opposition to the sectarian narrowness of Tertullian,[18] the fathers of the early church, from Justin Martyr to Origen and Augustine, have unanimously championed their conviction of the power of the divine word to germinate and spread, and of the presence of seeds of truth active in human history from the beginning in the folk wisdom of the different peoples and in the teaching of philosophers.

It is not, however, just its superhuman origin to which respect is due. We should not forget that the common possession of the sacred tradition creates a fundamental *unity* of all mankind, really a unity in relation to that foundation of spiritual life that—hidden but very real—first makes communication among human beings possible and worth attempting. It is really one of the most pernicious things happening on this planet that a secularizing global civilization, which seems to have its mind set on deserting and betraying definitively the basis of its great tradition, is compelling all remaining cultures to surrender their own *tradita* and so to uproot themselves. The result is that even the most heroic efforts to obtain a deeper "understanding" remain almost necessarily futile.

III

It is time to repeat our question. "Where" in the historical world of mankind can tradition be met with as a fact? Of the two "addresses" that we have given as answers so far, the second must necessarily remain much less definite than the first, but I did not want to suppress it for that reason. If there is a question about the reality of sacred tradition, it is really not possible to be silent about the myths of peoples. This same consideration, however, it seems to me, is true about the third address, although it is not much more than a hunch, and although in this case the concept of tradition may at most be realized in the manner of an analogy.

I am talking about definite certainties associated with the center of a person, which do not reveal themselves as themselves, admittedly, but whose presence and activity, under certain circumstances, are clearly visible. There may be reckoned among the most assured results of human depth psychology that—*first of all*—such normally unconscious "insights"[19] and "primordial ideas"[20] really exist and have as their object such basic facts as salvation, disaster, guilt, punishment, harmony, happiness. *Second*, although these basic assumptions are no more rationally demonstrable than the validity of the *tradita*, we are so completely certain of their truth that de facto we build our lives on them and become at odds with ourselves if we try to live otherwise. The *third* point is the most questionable, although it is of importance for our theme, namely that these convictions and ideas can possibly have the character of *tradita*. After all, it is C. G. Jung who explicitly uses the word "transmit" [*überliefern*] here.[21]

Of course, we must not think of this transmission as occurring through a personal act of sharing, but through a process of communication buried deep in what links the generations and hidden there. The way *hither* is by its very nature not available to the immediate perception of the recipient. Memory, however, traverses it *back*wards under certain conditions. This seems to be the purport of the platonic-Augustinian concept of *anámnesis—memoria*. As Gilson has convincingly demonstrated,[22] Augustine understands by "memory" not only something "trans-psychological," but also something super-individual, a power that allows one to pass over the succession of the generations and to recall experiences that have fallen to the lot of mankind in the early stages of its historical origin. How do we really know what a blissful life is? Do we not know because we remember it? This would mean that we were once blissful—perhaps in that man who was the first sinner? The Tenth Book of Augustine's *Confessions* turns these kinds of questions over and over again.[23] I am speaking here very tentatively, as I said, and with explicit reservations. Still, it is possible to justify mentioning these unconscious certainties which concern the whole of existence and are "assumed" without critical examination. They too are perhaps a "place" in which sacred tradition appears—although for our reflections it must remain less an area to be positively enlightened than one which must be left empty like a hollowed-out mold or a negative.

IV

From this last consideration it is only a short step to the question of the traditional character of *language*. Language is undoubtedly much more than a mere vehicle of tradition. It is itself a *traditum*—and not only in the sense that a definite stock of vocabulary with the grammar that accompanies it will be handed on from generation to generation. Words are always connected to an interpretation of world and reality that has already been stamped on them and which we simply take over without the possibility of their being articulated either by us or by the one who "hands it down" to us. Although here too, strictly speaking, there is no act of sharing and handing down, still we do not hesitate to speak of tradition. And right away we face the apparently insoluble problem of the *origin* of language. Fortunately, we do not need to enter upon that here. Still, we may be permitted to recall that according to Plato's opinion, it is "the ancients" who "give the names,"[24] just as the holy book of Christendom attributes to the earliest of mankind, Adam, the capacity to call all creatures by their names (Genesis 2:20).

It is necessary to point out right away that taking these opinions and stories seriously has nothing to do with "traditionalism." Nowadays, the term "traditionalism" is an overused term of abuse, which should properly be restricted to describing the nineteenth-century intellectual doctrine that taught that human reason by itself, i.e., without returning to the original revelation and tradition, is completely incapable of understanding the basic realities of existence. Clearly, it is possible to hold this formulation as totally false and at the same time to respect the sacred tradition as worthy of reverence and even as authoritative. And, obviously, neither point of view should be confused with a conservatism that indiscriminately resists all innovation. Of course, this conservatism really exists, as everybody knows. More than that, it seems to belong to one of the so-to-speak natural categories of decadence and risks against which everyone who accepts and assents to sacred tradition as a basic reality of history as it really occurs must arm himself from the start.

V

In the worldly conduct of this critical traditionalist there will always be a characteristic element of fundamental reverence and thankfulness, an explicit respect for what has grown to maturity and before the continuity of connections in life that concern more than the individual. What I am talking about here is too complex and too differentiated to allow for a simple and appropriate description and delimitation. Of course, I am not talking about the harmless uncritical naïveté that, when confronted with what in fact exists, thinks "whatever is, is good." I mean rather the selfless readiness to receive something that you could never pay for out of your own resources, and the modesty to know that you are in debt and at the same time in no position to pay that debt. I am talking about the "power of gratitude," the loss of which first really makes us disinherited.[25] This does not mean that a revolutionary attempt to grasp the purity of the legacy, the primeval form of the *tradita*, through all the "strata of interpretation"[26] that have been piled up in between, must be out of the question or ought to be. This origin, however, which throughout all history continues to contribute and be effective, remains always thankfully remembered and respected. Gabriel Marcel has interpreted this "encompassing gratitude" as consisting in recognizing and appreciating again (*re-connaissance*), as the attempt in a "mysterious restitution" to respond to what has been received without debt or obligation in tradition.[27]

To this "yes," this universal assent, there corresponds, like the flip side of a coin, a clear "no," or at least a very decisive distrust, for example, of the all-too-exclusive talk of the future—as though for human beings there was only something to hope for and nothing to remember and nothing to be thankful for. Respect for tradition produces distrust of that zero-point radicalism that fancies it always possible to start again from scratch with a *tabula rasa*, as well as distrust of the inclination to treat each new moment as a "completely new situation," and so forth. Against all this we shall have to take our stand on a very precise distinction. On one side belong such things as the "To boldly go where no man has gone before" of interplanetary travel, new discoveries in treating cancer, newly bred varieties of roses, progress in making cars and cameras. All this I can welcome without reservation and even expect with impatience. It is, however, a completely different matter when someone speaks to me enthusiastically of a "radically new" understanding of human nature, of a new interpretation of *eros* or death that replaces everything men have thought about them, of a completely new access to God's Word available for the first time to this generation, or of a completely changed conception of priesthood or sacrament. Then I immediately notice, before any discussion of individual points, a deep, unappeasable distrust rooted neither in some general will to stay in place nor in a principled rejection of "progress" but in the well-founded suspicion that in this area, to use Karl Jaspers's expression, "novelty can speak against truth."[28] "In this area" means wherever we are dealing with the whole of the world and reality; wherever the particulars of the sacred tradition are being proclaimed; wherever important topics are beyond the clutches of the exact sciences.

Two things are part and parcel of the nature of science: it does not ask questions about the total coherence of life, and tradition has no place in it. Four hundred years before Pascal, Albertus Magnus had already expressed this point with aggressive decisiveness. When the question is whether the dolphin is a fish or not, he does not ask Aristotle or the "ancients" at all. *Experimentum solum certificat in talibus.* In such matters experience alone brings certainty.[29] This is why it is imprecise and misleading to call modern science "fundamentally tradition-less," or to say that the rise of modern science already presupposes a "break with tradition."[30] In this regard there is no difference in principle between ancient and modern experimental science. Where there is no marriage, there is no adultery. Philosophy and its relation to tradition stand on a completely different footing than science.

CHAPTER 6

SACRED TRADITION AND PHILOSOPHY: INCLUSION OF THE *TRADITA*

I

Of course, in its basic structure the philosophical act is completely different from the act of handing down a tradition. This was also the opinion of ancient philosophy. Aristotle has been interpreted as though for him "First Philosophy" remains "Theology," "because it has the mission of transmitting the knowledge of the divine which is always appropriate for human beings."[1] I believe that it can be convincingly demonstrated that this opinion rests on an erroneous interpretation. There are two reasons why "First Philosophy" is the most divine of the sciences, according to Aristotle's *Metaphysics*:[2] (1) because its ultimate mission is to investigate God, and (2) because God possesses it most completely. Therefore, admittedly, a special relationship to the sacred tradition is, if not exactly asserted, still prepared and suggested. The question of the nature of this relationship remains an open one.

It is striking that Pascal's thesis on the value of tradition, which we discussed near the beginning of this book, has not a word to say about philosophy. Physics' relationship to tradition, on the one hand, and theology's, on the other, are basically unproblematic and clear. Physics has absolutely nothing to do with tradition, while theology can actually be defined as the "science of tradition," that is, as the attempt to interpret what was really meant in the utterances of God embodied in the *tradita*. In practice, this interpretation is a task of almost overwhelming difficulty. The progress of research into the world and mankind through science, precisely in order to preserve the living presence of the *tradita*, which do not change, requires reformulations that must be continually corrected, worked on, and made more precise in a debate that is open to many voices and excludes in principle no argument and no participant. This debate, when it is really conducted and sustained, belongs to the most exciting events in intellectual history. And it is not theology alone that profits by this debate. Although naturally the *tradita* have no voice in its internal process of decision-making about content, science, too, benefits to a certain extent—from the outside, one might say, because the opposition of tradition compels greater discretion and a definite direction of attention.[3] Still, these complications do not affect the structure of the act of theology, which is in principle completely transparent, nor the unambiguous character of its relationship to the sacred tradition.

What, however, is the situation with philosophy? When I say "philosophy," I mean by that name not a specialized academic discipline, but rather an activity that belongs to the basic elements of any intellectual existence. No intellectual existence can renounce or repudiate it, and no one who desires or claims to lead an intellectual life can dispense with it. This activity, as has become clear, does not consist either in simply receiving by hearing something handed down and then handing it down again, or in interpreting a *traditum*. It never occurred to me to explain "philosophy as the practice of tradition."[4] For me, philosophizing is reflecting on the whole of what meets us in experience from every possible aspect in its fundamental significance.[5] A person who practices philosophy therefore is not so much a deep thinker who has formulated a well-rounded worldview as it is anyone who keeps a question open and thinks it through methodically.

II

How, then, does this kind of questioner succeed in dealing with tradition, especially sacred tradition? We ought to admit that he will not succeed in dealing with it at all—unless he stands *as a person* in a tradition and participates in it as a believing hearer. But is this not the same thing as saying that tradition really does not concern me "as" a practitioner of philosophy? No, it is not at all the same thing! Rather it means the following. After and insofar as I as a person am actually participating in a tradition, or, to put it another way, insofar as I actually accept the *tradita* of sacred tradition as truth for whatever reasons (but of course not uncritically or arbitrarily), then and only then do I have the capacity to practice philosophy seriously, i.e., to reflect on my subject under any possible consideration, if I include the information that has been explicitly handed down within the discussions. This is just as true for a Greek of the time of Socrates as for a contemporary Christian. It was precisely the great founders of Western philosophizing who confronted explicitly rational argumentation with the mythological tradition. And if the reader who is born much later still tastes the salt of the existential in the platonic *Symposium*, the reason is that Plato in the discussion of the question about the essence of Eros opens the floor not only to biology, psychology, and sociology, but also to those who interpret the myth of mankind's original perfection and fall: you can understand nothing of what Eros is and means, he seems to say, if you do not include in your reflections this primitive experience of mankind; if you do not recognize that all erotic desire is in the final analysis nothing else than hunting for mankind's healthy original form.

Obviously, the formulation "inclusion of the *tradita*" refers to an extremely complicated procedure, but this is not the place to discuss even the more relevant details. We are dealing, however, with bringing what is known and believed into a contrapuntal relationship of such a nature that, on the one hand, the independence of both remains clearly preserved, while on the other hand, on the basis of reciprocal corroboration, challenge, and perhaps even disturbance there arises a new and richer harmony, which is much more than the mere addition of the basic elements.

The existential impetus, authenticity, depth, and (so to speak) stout-heartedness of the act of philosophizing is dependent on whether or not this contrapuntal relationship to the sacred tradition is realized or not. How true this is, I would like to make clear experimentally by means of an example of contrasts that made a deep impression on me. I am going to use a historical experiment, which perhaps can only be observed in our West European civilization and society. I have long cherished admiration and respect for the historical learning of Japanese professors of philosophy. They know their Hegel or Heidegger or Sartre with the sovereign command of specialists, and when asked about the most obscure individual questions, they respond with totally precise and informative answers. Such detailed knowledge, however, cannot be the basis of real philosophizing for very long. When a Westerner tries to discuss basic philosophical problems with these experts, not "what other people have thought, but how the true nature of things actually stands,"[6] he soon sees that no matter how extremely well versed these experts are in Western terminology, their responses exhibit a disjointedness that seems almost creepy, like the artificial liveliness of marionettes. In my opinion, there is no reason to be surprised at this. All of Western philosophy maintains its vitality by nourishing itself on the conversation—perhaps I really ought to have said, the debate—with the sacred tradition of Christendom that precedes it. This relationship of philosophy with the Christian tradition is not always obvious, and for anyone who does not notice it, the atheism of Jean-Paul Sartre is necessarily just as inaccessible as Martin Heidegger's ontology of Nothing and Death. Even when this sacred partnership is thoroughly understood, it cannot be simply transported to the soil of a fundamentally different culture.

I was once a guest in Tokyo at one of those dinner parties that go on for hours, and late in the evening I asked a question of my enlightened colleagues: could they describe to me the pre-philosophical sacred tradition on the basis of which a distinctively Japanese way of philosophizing could develop contrapuntally? The immediate response was a lengthy and apparently lively dispute, carried on by my dinner companions in their mother tongue, of which the European dinner guest understood not a word. When I vigorously interrupted their discussion, I finally received the reply that they were debating whether or not there was a "mythical tradition" of a specifically Japanese stamp at all, and, if so, what it was like. My initial suspicion, that a genuinely Japanese philosophy was to be sought most likely in the cloisters of Zen Buddhism or the temples of Shinto, seemed to me rather confirmed than refuted.

If we take a look at contemporary European philosophy from the same point of view, the most characteristic thing about it, which forces itself on our attention, is precisely the process of the increasingly coherent elimination of the *tradita* from the circle of philosophical discussion. We find here too—perhaps we should say, here most of all—confirmation of the diagnosis that Friedrich Nietzsche wrote down about 1890: "What is under the most profound attack today is the instinct and will of tradition. All institutions which owe their origin to this instinct are opposed to the taste of the modern intellect."[7]

Of course, this sentence aims at much more than the field of philosophy. It was coined first and foremost for another purpose. It is surely valid, for example, in the area of the arts. The power of the musical arts to entrance us and move us deeply is nourished by that dimension of reality which is revealed in tradition. And by "tradition" here I mean explicitly not just any stock of customary matters, whether in form or content, but rather "*sacred* tradition" in the strict sense. Anybody who finds this statement too farfetched or too "pious" might want to hear the same opinion from Goethe in his old age. In a letter to Zelter stands this astounding sentence: "Every true artist should be seen as one who wants to preserve something that is recognized as holy and to propagate it seriously and prudently. Every century, however, according to its nature aspires to the secular and seeks to make the holy common, the difficult easy and the serious fun. I would have no objection to this, except that it ends up ruining both seriousness and fun."[8]

III

At any rate, in philosophy, which is here our only concern, for some considerable time now philosophers have violently and on principle been "aspiring to the secular." We might want to add that we "would have no objection to this," except that it "ends up ruining" the goal and purpose of philosophy. This is true not just of philosophy but of mankind's entire intellectual and spiritual way of life.

The exclusion of the "sacred tradition" from the practice of philosophizing can occur in two ways, it seems. The first is by the destruction of its content and its replacement by a kind of anti-tradition. A perfect example of this is Jean-Paul Sartre, who bases his philosophy explicitly on the dogma of the nonexistence of God. From a purely formal point of view, Sartre has preserved completely the contrapuntal ordering of the known to the believed. I am convinced that this is the reason for the perplexing existential relevance of Sartre's philosophizing. It is a clear example of that "inclusion" of fundamental positions which concern the whole of reality and must be assumed without critical examination as the presuppositions for rational thought. My one reservation is that this purely negative dogmatics is admittedly proclaiming its opposition to all sacred tradition.

There is, however, another, even more effective way of silencing the *tradita* in the field of philosophy: by denying not the content, but rather the formal structure of the contrapuntal ordering itself. According to the program of "Scientific Philosophy," for instance, philosophers are supposed simply to stop reflecting on the whole of world and reality from any possible aspect. Instead, they are supposed to limit themselves, like physicists, to the questions of their academic specialty, and then to solve them with verifiable results. Of course, in such academic fields the occasion for an appeal to tradition, whether sacred or profane, arises just as little as it does in physics. At any rate, philosophy—still called by this name—turns unavoidably into a business that can only be pursued by specialists and is in fact of no interest to anybody else. The place that belongs to philosophy and the philosophizer in the whole of existence remains empty.

"Empty" is also the word used by two important philosophical critics of our time to describe the intellectual condition created by such a consciously tradition-less philosophy. (They are philosophically very far apart and certainly used the word independently of one another.) One is Karl Jaspers, who with his eye on a widely influential figure of contemporary philosophy says that the contents of the "Great Tradition," without which philosophy must inevitably die out and disappear,[9] have been abandoned, and that the result is "an increasingly empty seriousness."[10] I have quoted several times Viacheslav Ivanov, the "Western Russian,"[11] scholar of myth, humanist, and philosopher. Confronted by the liberal historian, who is hysterically rejoicing in the good fortune of bathing in the stream of the river Lethe in order to wash away every memory of religion, philosophy, and poetry and then walk to the shore as naked as the first man,[12] he answers with the decisive judgment: "Freedom achieved by forgetting is empty."[13]

IV

Another aspect of the catastrophe that threatens the intellectual community of mankind because of the loss of knowledge of sacred tradition was expressed by one of the last essays written by Gerhard Krüger before the silence that he has maintained for many years now. The essay contains the frightening sentence: "The only reason we are still alive is our inconsistency in not having actually silenced all tradition.[14] . . . We are facing the radical impossibility of a meaningful common existence, although no one can imagine what this end would be like."[15] Anyone who is inclined to consider this statement as an excessively gloomy cry from a modern-day Cassandra should reflect that we are dealing with a very precise assertion, which has nothing to do with the literary genre of uncivil criticism of the present or a vague philosophy of decadence. Krüger is alluding, with complete seriousness, to the unifying power of tradition. He is pointing out that the decisive unity of the human race cannot be based on or guaranteed by realizing a political "One World" or any kind of unanimity of "cultural wills," no, not by a shared respect before art and science, not by the technical possibilities of communication throughout the planet earth, not by a universal world language, whether it be English or Esperanto or Chinese, not even by international organizations for athletic competition. Rather, real unity among human beings has its roots in nothing else but the common possession of tradition in the strict sense—I mean, our sharing in common the sacred tradition that goes back to God's words.

NOTES

TRANSLATOR'S PREFACE

1. Josef Pieper, *Noch nicht aller Tage Abend* (München, 1979), 96 = *Werke* EB 2.310.

2. "Über die Schlichtheit der Sprache in der Philosophie," the epilogue to C. S. Lewis, *Über den Schmerz*, Hildegard und Josef Pieper, trans., (Köln, 1954), 185–92.

3. "Über die Schlichtheit der Sprache in der Philosophie," *Tradition als Herausforderung* (München, 1963), 286–94.

4. Josef Pieper, "On Clarity," *Chronicles* 12.4 (April 1988), 12–13 = "Sprechen über das *mirandum*," *Werke* 8,1.224–27.

5. *Noch wußte es niemand* (München, 1976), 53–54 = *No One Could Have Known* (San Francisco, 1987), 48 = *Werke* EB 2.62–63 and *Philosophie in Selbstdarstellung* (Hamburg, 1975), 241–42 = *Werke* EB 2.1–2.

6. *Von Sinn der Tapferkeit* (Leipzig, 1934) = *Werke* 4.113–36

7. *Fortitude and Temperance* (New York, 1954).

8. Josef Pieper, *Werke* in 8 Bänden, Berthold Wald, ed. (Hamburg, 1995–2007) and 2 Ergangzungsbände (Hamburg 2004–5). These last two volumes are cited by me as EB 1 and 2.

9. *Noch nicht aller Tage Abend*, 97 = *Werke* EB 2.310–11.

10. *Was kann uns heute Tradition bedeutet?* (Mainz, 1997)

11. "Was heißt 'Christliche Abendland,'" *Tradition als Herausforderung* (München, 1963), 36–47. The quotations appear on p. 37.

12. Josef Pieper, *For the Love of Wisdom: Essays on the Nature of Philosophy*, Edited by Berthold Wald, Translated by Roger Wasserman (San Francisco, 2006).

TRANSLATOR'S INTRODUCTION

1. Josef Pieper, "On Clarity," *Chronicles* 12.4 (April 1988), 12–13 = "Sprechen über das mirandum," *Werke* 8,1.224–27, a translation of part of the epilogue, entitled "Über die Schlichtheit der Sprache in der Philosophie," to a translation of C. S. Lewis, *The Problem of Pain* by Hildegard and Josef Pieper, *Über den Schmerz* (Köln, 1954), 191–92 = *Tradition als Herausforderung* (München, 1963), 286–94.

2. Josef Pieper, *Leisure: The Basis of Culture* (New York, 1952), a translation of *Muße und Kult* (München, 1948) = *Werke* 6.1–44 and *Was heißt Philosophieren* (München, 1948) = *Werke* 3.15–70.

3. Thomas Fleming, "Homage to T. S. Eliot," *Chronicles* 12.4 (April 1988), 9.

4. *Human All Too Human*, I.9.552: "The only human right.—The man who diverges from the traditional is the victim of the unusual; the one who remains in the traditional is its slave. In either event he is ruined."

5. Josef Pieper, *Überlieferung. Begriff und Anspruch* (München, 1970), 109.

6. Josef Pieper, *Über den Begriff der Tradition* (Köln-Opladen, 1958).

7. "Tradition in der sich wandelnden Welt," *Tradition als Herausforderung*, 11–35 = *Werke* 8,1.184–99.

8. "Gewährdung und Bewahrung der Tradition," *Was Wird aus dem Menschen*, Otto Schatz, ed. (Graz/Wien/Köln, 1974), 159–81 = *Werke* 7.188–209.

9. *Was kann uns heute Tradition bedeuten?* (Mainz, 1997).

10. "Herkunftslose Zukunft und Hoffnung ohne Grund?" *Über die Schwierigkeit heute zu glauben* (München, 1974), 178–95 = *Problems of Modern Faith* (Chicago, 1984), 157–73 = *Werke* 7.344–56

11. Theodor W. Adorno, "Thesen über Tradition," *Ohne Leitbild* (Franfurt am Main, 1967), 35 ["Über" Tradition, *Gesammelte Schriften* 10.1 (Frankfurt am Main, 1977), 315 = "On Tradition" *Telos* 94 (Winter 1993–1994), 78].

12. Max Horkheimer and Theodor W. Adorno, *Dialektik der Aufklärung* (Amsterdam, 1947) = *Dialectic of Enlightenment* (New York, 1972).

13. Josef Pieper, *Über den Begriff der Tradition*, 54

14. Pieper typically included Kant among the philosophers who valued sacred

tradition, citing Kant's letter to Heinrich Jung-Schiller in 1789, "It is quite right of you to seek in the Gospels the final satisfaction of your striving for a secure foundation of wisdom and hope, since that book is an everlasting guide to true wisdom, one that not only agrees with the speculations of a perfected reason but sheds new light on the whole field surveyed by that reason, illuminating what still remains opaque to it." For the first draft, *Kant's gesammelte Schriften* XI (Berlin/Leipzig) 10 = *Kant: Philosophical Correspondence 1759–99*, Arnulf Zweig, ed. (Chicago, 1967), 131; for the letter Kant sent, *Kant's gesammelte Schriften* XXIII (Berlin, 1955), 494–95 = *Immanuel Kant: Correspondence*, Arnulf Zweig, ed. (Cambridge, 1999) 289–91. Pieper quotes the sentence at *Scholasticism* (New York, 1960), 13 = *Scholastik* (München, 1960), 15 = *Werke* 2.302 and *Verteidigungsrede für Philosophie* (München, 1966), 132 = *In Defense of Philosophy* (San Francisco, 1992), 117 = *Werke* 3.152–53.

15. Hans-Georg Gadamer, *Die Aktualität des Schönen* (Stuttgart, 1977), 42–46 = *The Relevance of the Beautiful and Other Essays*, translated by Nicholas Walker (Cambridge, 1986), 31–35.

16. *Leisure*, 116 = *Werke* 3.60–61.

17. John Rawls, *A Theory of Justice* (Cambridge, MA, 1971); Charles Taylor, *Hegel* (Cambridge, 1975).

18. Charles Taylor, *A Catholic Modernity* (New York/Oxford, 1999).

19. Charles Taylor, "Geschlossene Weltstrukturen in der Moderne," *Wissen und Weisheit* (Dokumentationen der Josef Pieper Stiftung, Band 6) (Münster, 2005), 137–69.

20. Alasdair MacIntyre, *After Virtue*: *A Study in Moral Theory* (Notre Dame, 1981, 1984[2]); *Whose Justice? Which Rationality?* (Notre Dame, 1988); *Three Rival Versions of Moral Inquiry*: *Encyclopaedia, Genealogy and Tradition* (Notre Dame, 1990).

21. Christopher Stephen Lutz, *Tradition in the Ethics of Alasdair MacIntyre* (Lanham, MD, 2004).

22. *Whose Justice? Which Rationality?* 164–82.

23. *Philosophie in Selbstdarstellungen* I (Hamburg, 1975), 241 = *Werke* EB 2.1.

24. *No One Could Have Known* (San Francisco, 1987), 46 = *Noch Wußte es Niemand* (München, 1976), 51 = *Werke* EB 2.60 (*cartesianisch gefärbte Rationalität*).

25. E.g., *Über die Schwierigkeit*, 181 = *Problems*, 160 = *Werke* 7.346.

26. Thomas Fleming, *The Politics of Human Nature* (New Brunswick, NJ, 1988), 204.

27. Josef Pieper, *Neuordnung der menschlichen Gesellschaft: Befreiung des Proletariats/ Berufständische Gliederung, Systematische Einführung in die Enzyklika* Quadragesimo Anno (Frankfurt am Main, 1932) = *Werke* EB 1.61–141. Subsidiarity is discussed at 88–89 = 126.

28. Werner Jaeger, *Aristoteles. Grundlegung einer Geschichte seiner Entwicklung* (Berlin, 1923) = *Aristotle. Fundamentals of the History of His Development* (Oxford, 1934). Pieper describes meeting Jaeger at *Noch nicht aller Tage Abend* (München, 1979), 105 = *Werke* EB 2.318.

29. *Über das Ende der Zeit* (München, 1950), 63 = *The End of Time* (New York, 1954), 54 = *Werke* 6.314. Similar comments are found at *Vertidigungsrede*, 131 = *In Defense*, 117 = *Werke* 3.152 and the unpublished manuscript, "Über das Dilemma einer nicht-christlichen Philosophie" (1950), *Werke* 3.304.

30. *Aristoteles*, 404 = *Aristotle*, 378.

31. *Scholastik*, 39 = *Scholasticism*, 30 = *Werke* 2.316.

32. G. E. L. Owen, *Logic, Science, and Dialectic* (Ithaca, NY, 1986); Wolfgang Kullmann, *Wissenschaft und Methode* (Berlin, 1974); *Aristoteles und die moderne Wissenschaft* (Stuttgart, 1998).

33. Whose *Justice? Which Rationality?* 94.

34. John M. Rist, *On Inoculating Moral Philosophy against God* (Milwaukee, WI, 1999), 27.

35. Arbogast Schmitt, *Die Moderne und Platon* (Stuttgart, 2003).

36. *Leisure*, 112 = *Werke* 3.57.

37. *Scholasticism* (New York, 1960), 126 = *Scholastik* (München, 1960), 171 = *Werke* 2.404.

38. Alasdair MacIntyre, *After Virtue* (1981), 206 = (1984), 222.

39. G. S. Kirk, J. E. Raven, M. Schofield, *The Pre-Socratic Philosophers* (Cambridge, 1983²), 82, 92–93.

40. Charles H. Kahn, *Pythagoras and the Pythagoreans* (Indianapolis, 2001), 153–72.

41. Eugene Wigner, "The Unreasonable Effectiveness of Mathematics in the Natural Sciences," *Communications in Pure and Applied Mathematics* 13.1 (February 1960) = *Symmetries and Reflections* (Bloomington, IN, 1967), 222–37.

42. Josef Pieper, "On Clarity," *Chronicles* 12.4 (April 1988), 13 = "Sprechen über das *mirandum*," *Werke* 8,1.227 (*unergründlich*).

43. John Barrow, *The World within the World* (Oxford, 1988), vii, lists seven "traditional unspoken assumptions on which modern science is based."

44. I have modified the translation in *The Born-Einstein Letters: Friendship, Politics and Physics in Uncertain Times* (Basingstoke/New York, 1972, 2005²), 88, of Albert Einstein–Hedwig und Max Born, *Briefwechsel 1916–1955* (München, 1969), 129–30.

45. Josef Pieper, *Scholastik* (München, 1960), 241, n. 35 = *Scholasticism* (New York, 1960), 181, n. 35 = *Werke*, 2.395, n. 276.

46. Albertus Magnus, *De Animalibus Libri XXVI*. Hermann Stadler, ed., II (Munster, 1920), 1525 = *On Animals. A Medieval* Summa Zoologica, translated and annotated by Kenneth F. Kitchell and Irven Michael Resnick II (Baltimore, 1999), 1671.

47. Lynn Thorndike, *A History of Magic and Experimental Science* II (New York, 1923), 528–48, esp. 539–42.

48. Michael Polanyi, *Science, Faith, and Society*, Riddell Memorial Lectures, Eighteenth Series (London, 1946); Karl Popper, "Towards a Rational Theory of Tradition," *Rationalist Annual* (1948) 36–55 = *Conjectures and Refutations* (London, 1962), 120–35.

49. Edward Shils, *Tradition* (London: Faber and Faber, 1981), 100–114, with bibliography at n. 24, p. 101, including Werner Heisenberg, "Tradition in Science," *Tradition in Science* (New York, 1983).

50. Aristotle, *Parts of Animals* I.5

51. G. E. Lloyd, *Aristotle: The Growth and Structure of His Thought* (Cambridge, 1968), 86–90. Pierre Pellegrin, *Aristotle's Classification of Animals* (Berkeley, CA, 1986) does not question Aristotle's influence.

52. Aristotle, *Generation of Animals* III.10.760b29–33.

53. "Was ist eine Kirche?" *Über die Schwierigkeit*, 123 = *Problems*, 103 = *Werke* 7.550.

54. "This is my body," found at Matthew 26:26, Mark 14:22, Luke 22:19, I Corinthians 11:24. "In such matters only God's word brings certainty," in reference to Albert's words, quoted above.

55. Isaac Newton, *The Principia* (Berkeley, CA, 1999), 940 = *Isaac Newton's Philosophiae Naturalis Principia Mathematica* II (Cambridge, MA, 1972), 760.

CHAPTER 1

1. ["World history is the progress of the consciousness of freedom." G. W. F. Hegel, *Vorlesungen über die Philosophie der Weltgeschichte*, Johannes Hoffmeister, ed., I: *Einleitung: Die Vernunft in der Geschichte* (Leipzig, 1955), 63 = *Lectures on the Philosophy of World History: Introduction: Reason in History*, translated by H. B. Nisbet (Cambridge, 1975), 54.]

2. [Pieper first heard this expression from Professor Johann Plenge in 1928 as part of an interpretation of the essential identity of communism and fascism, *Noch Wußte Es Niemand* (München, 1979), 86–87 = *No One Could Have Known* (San Francisco, 1987), 78 = *Werke* EB 2.91. Pieper, writing on "the social ideal and labor," *Pharus* 25 (1934), 273 = *Werke* EB 1.374 attributed "the classic formulation" of this idea to Ernst

Jünger's *Der Arbeiter. Herrschaft und Gestalt* (Hamburg, 1932; Stuttgart, 1981). One of the major targets of *Leisure: The Basis of Culture* (New York, 1952) = *Muße und Kult* (München, 1948) = *Werke* 6.1–44, Jünger predicted that the important nineteenth-century concept, the bourgeois individual, will be replaced by the worker, who, neither individual nor mass man, will be the central figure in a new society devoted to "total mobilization" (the title of an essay by Jünger, *Totale Mobilmachung*), like the draft in World War I. ("Mobilization through a general draft will be replaced by a total or work mobilization" [302] in "entire work armies" [*ganze Arbeitsheere*, 304].)]

3. ["Das Wort sie sollen lassen stahn," the first line of the fourth stanza of Martin Luther's famous hymn, "Ein' feste Burg," "A Mighty Fortress."]

4. *Œuvres de Blaise Pascal*, L. Brunschvicg et P. Boutroux, eds., II (Paris, 1908), 129–45 [= Pascal, *Œuvres Complètes*, Louis Lafuma, ed., (Paris, 1963), 230–32 = Pascal, *Œuvres Complètes*, Michel Le Guern, ed., I (Paris, 1998), 452–58 = Emile Cailliet and John C. Blankenagel, trans., *Great Shorter Works of Pascal* (Philadephia, 1948), 50–55].

5. For the details, see Ersch-Gruber, *Allgemeine Enzyklopädie der Wissenschaften und Künste*, Band III (Leipzig, 1839), 486 ff.; [Richard S. Westfall, *The Construction of Modern Science: Mechanisms and Mechanics* (London, 1971; second edition, Cambridge, 1977), 43–48; John D. Barrow, *The Book of Nothing* (London/New York, 2000), 89–114].

6. [=Brunschvicg/Boutroux 153 = Lafuma 221 = Le Guern 427 = Cailliet/Blankenagel 56 (Letter of Pascal to M. Périer, November 15, 1647).]

7. Descartes wrote in *Principia Philosophiae* (1644), "We understand very clearly" (*perspicue intelligimus*) that there is a kind of matter which fills completely every imaginable space. Its nature consists "in this alone, that it is an extended substance....We find in ourselves absolutely no idea of any other kind of matter." *Principia Philosophiae* II.22 [*Œuvres de Descartes*, Charles Adam and Paul Tannery, eds., VIIIA (Paris, 1905), 52; *Philosophical Writings of Descartes*, John Cottingham, Robert Stoothoff, and Dugald Murdoch, trans.. I (Cambridge, 1885), 232] Similar comments are found in *Metéores* [Meteorology], Discours I [Adam/Tannery VI (Paris, 1902), 233–38].

8. [=Brunschvicg/Boutroux 154–55 = Lafuma 222 = Le Guern 427 = Cailliet/Blankenagle 56.]

9. [=Brunschvicg/Boutroux 155 = Lafuma 222 = Le Guern 427; mistranslated by Cailliet/Blankenagel 57.]

10. The problem of the existence of a void was already discussed in pre-Socratic philosophy. The void is denied in the late platonic dialogue *Timaeus* 79b1; 79c1.

The medieval commentators on Aristotle devote considerable space to the question, e.g., Thomas Aquinas, *In Physica* 4 [.9–14 = *Opera Omnia* 2 (Rome, 1884), 173–96 = *Commentary on Aristotle's Physics*, translated by Richard J. Blackwell et al. (New Haven, CT, 1963), 223–51]. Aquinas includes the arguments of Averroes as well [*In Physica* 4.12,] nr. 535–37 [= *Opera Omnia* 2, 4.12.9–11 (pp. 186–87) = *Commentary*, 238–40. See Edward Grant, *Much Ado About Nothing: Theories of Space and Vacuum from the Middle Ages to the Scientific Revolution* (Cambridge, 1981).]

11. Brunschvicg/Boutroux 129 [= Lafuma 230 = Le Guern 452 = Cailliet/Blankenagel 50]. See also [his letters to Père Noël, October 29, 1647 (Brunschvicg/Boutroux 90–106 = Lafuma 200–204 = Le Guern 377–86 = Cailliet/Blankenagel 42–50) and Le Pailleur, February or March, 1648 (Brunschvicg/Boutroux 179–211 = Lafuma 208–15 = Le Guern 396–412 = Cailliet/Blankenagel 61–76).]

12. Brunschvicg/Boutroux 129[–30 = Lafuma 230 = Le Guern 452 = Cailliet/Blankenagel 50].

13. Pascal names along with theology also history, geography, jurisprudence, and languages [Brunschvicg/Boutroux 130 = Lafuma 230 = Le Guern 452 = Cailliet/Blankenagel 51]. With physics he adduces geometry, music, and architecture [Brunschvicg/Boutroux 132 = Lafuma 230 = Le Guern 453 = Cailliet/Blankenagel 52]. As he develops his argument he speaks only of theology, on the one hand, and physics, on the other.

14. Brunschvicg/Boutroux 141 [= Lafuma 232 = Le Guern 456–57 = Cailliet/Blankenagel 54].

15. Brunschvicg/Boutroux 133 [= Lafuma 231 = Le Guern 454 = Cailliet/Blankenagel 52. Pieper uses the German word, *Verwirrung*, "confusion," to translate the French word *Malheur*, "misfortune"].

16. Brunschvicg/Boutroux 145 [= Lafuma 232 = Le Guern 458 = Cailliet/Blankenagel 55].

17. For example, those of Walter Brugger [*Philosophische Wörterbuch*, translated by Kenneth Baker as *Philosophical Dictionary* (Spokane, WA, 1972)]; Johann Hoffmeister [*Wörterbuch der philosophischen Begriffe* (Hamburg, 1955²)]; Rudolf Eisler [*Wörterbuch der philosophischen Begriffe und Ausdrücke* (Berlin, 1899). This lacuna has been filled by Volker Steenblock, "Tradition," *Historisches Wörterbuch der Philosophie*, 10 (Basel, 1998) 1315–29, a revision of Eisler at first edited by Joachim Ritter].

18. *Dictionnaire de Théologie Catholique*, volume 15.1, 1253.

19. [Friedrich Büchsel, "paradosis," *Theologisches Wörterbuch zum Neuen Testament* 2 (Stuttgart, 1935),174–75 = *Theological Dictionary of the New Testament*, Gerhard

Kittel, ed., translated by Geoffrey W. Bromily, 2 (Grand Rapids, MI, 1964), 172–73.]

20. [Arnold Ehrhardt, "Traditio," *Paulys Real-Encyclopädie der classischen Altertumswissenschaft* II.6 (1937), 1875–92.]

21. Rudolph Sohm, *Institutionen. Geschichte und System des römischen Privatrechts* (Leipzig, 1905¹²), 309 [= *The Institutes: A Textbook of the History and System of Roman Private Law* (Oxford, 1907³), 312].

CHAPTER 2

1. "In what follows the [German] nouns *Tradition* and *Überlieferung* will be used as meaning the same thing." [I have omitted this sentence from the main text.]

2. Gerhard Krüger, *Geschichte und Tradition* (Stuttgart 1948), 22 for the first quotation; the second is found at Gerhard Krüger, "Die Bedeutung der Tradition für die philosophische Forschung," *Studium Generale* 4 (1951), 321. [Both articles are reprinted in Gerhard Krüger, *Freiheit und Weltverwaltung. Aufsätze zur Philosophie der Geschichte* (Freiburg/München, 1958), 88; 213.]

3. Gerhard Krüger, *Geschichte und Tradition*, 13 [= 78].

4. [e.g., *Alcibiades* I.119b1, 124b10; *Gorgias* 506a4; *Laches* 196c8, 187d; *Meno* 86c5; *Philebus* 26e2; *Protagoras* 330b6.]

5. Plato, *Theaetetus* 198b.

6. August Deneffe, *Der Traditionsbegriff* (Münster in Westfalen, 1931), 7–8. An entire chapter of this book has the title "Tradere equals teaching" (7).

7. See Josef Pieper, *Über den Glauben* (München, 1962), 26–27 [= *Belief and Faith* (New York, 1963), 12–15 = *Werke* 4.202–7].

8. August Deneffe says in his very clear and enlightening study of the concept of tradition that it is no part "of the concept of tradition that something which is received will be handed on" (pp. 13 and 5). For this he appeals to the words of Jesus, *omnia mihi tradita sunt a Patre meo* (Matthew 11:27). I would say to this that naturally here, too, in the case of *tradere,* we are dealing with an improper use of the word. Of course, there are passages in the Bible where *tradere* means little more than "give away" and "deliver." Insofar as German [and English] are concerned, the words of Jesus cited by Deneffe could hardly be correctly translated by "hand down" [*überliefern*], but rather by "hand over" [*übertragen*] or "deliver" [*übergeben*].

9. I Corinthians 11:23; 15:3.

10. *Contra Julianum* 2.10.34; Migne, *Patrologia Latina* 44, 698.

11. [Pieper quotes the sentence in English. He tells this story from his 1962 trip to India under the heading "Dead Tradition" in *Noch Nicht Aller Tage Abend* (München, 1979), 233–34 = *Werke* EB 2.429–30.]

12. Leopold Ziegler, *Menschwerdung*, Band I (Olten 1948) 46 cites this expression from Paul Vulliaud, *La clé traditionelle des Évangiles*. [It is quoted in Aramaic (not Hebrew), transliterated and translated on the title page, where it is attributed to the tractate *Yoma*, the fifth section of the second major division of the Talmud of Babylonia, which is devoted to the major festivals. *Yoma* is Aramaic for "Day," *scilicet* "of Atonement." The sentence is cited and discussed by Marcus Jastrow, *A Dictionary of the Targumim, the Talmud Babli and Yerushalmi, and the Midrashic Literature* (New York, 1950), 255b: "to remember well something old (to refresh the memory) is more difficult than to commit it to memory." Jacob Neusner, *The Talmud of Babylonia. An Academic Commentary* V (Atlanta, 1994), 100, translates: "It is harder to remember well what is long familiar than to memorize something new, the analogy being cement made of old cement." In an e-mail posting Professor Neusner says the Aramaic "closely rendered yields 'learning in ancient matters is harder than in new ones.'" He goes on to comment, "Pieper's citation is pretty close to the Aramaic, an old teaching is harder than a new teaching. But that does not have any obvious meaning."]

13. It is at least problematic to define tradition as "the capacity to preserve and hand down non-informational knowledge," Leszek Kolakowski, "Von Sinn der Tradition," *Merkur* 23.12 (December 1969), 1086 [= "Der Anspruch auf die selbstverschuldete Unmündigkeit," in Leonhard Reinisch, ed., *Von Sinn der Tradition* (München, 1970), 2 = "On the Meaning of Tradition," *Evergreen Review* v. 15, no. 88 (April 1971), 43.]

14. Karl Jaspers, *Von der Wahrheit* (München, 1947), 838.

15. Joachim Ritter in his response to Josef Pieper, *Begriff der Tradition*, 47.

16. "In fact, it is the real paradox of the situation of historical thinking in the nineteenth century, that, on the one hand, it preserves memory, which, on the other hand, it dissolves . . . ; that historicism, on the one hand, wants to hand down, but, on the other, threatens . . . this tradition." Theodor Schieder in his response to Josef Pieper, *Begriff der Tradition*, 43.

17. Gerhard Krüger, *Bedeutung der Tradition*, 325 [= 223]; see also 322 [= 215]. Also Joachim Ritter, "Aristoteles und die Vorsokratiker," *Felsefe Arkivi* [Istanbul] 3 (1954) 21 [= *Metaphysik und Politik. Studien zu Aristoteles und Hegel* (Frankfurt am Main, 1969), 40].

18. *Gorgias* 523a.

19. *Phaedo* 114d1.

20. *Phaedo* 114d6.

21. Aristotle, *Sophistic Refutations* 2.2 [165b3].

22. Josef Pieper, "Platonische Figuren: Die Lernenden," *Tradition als Herausforderung* (München, 1963), 269–82 [= Werke 1.212–20].

23. Alexander Rüstow, "Kulturtradition und Kulturkritik," *Studium Generale* 4 (1951), 308.

24. Rüstow, 308.

25. Wilhelm Bacher, *Tradition und Tradenten in den Schulen Palästinas und Babyloniens* (Leipzig, 1914), 20.

26. [V. S. Soloviev, *The Heart of Reality: Essays on Beauty, Love, and Ethics* (Notre Dame, IN, 2003), 130].

27. Wjatscheslaw Iwanow, *Das Alte Wahre. Essays* (Frankfurt am Main, 1954), 160.

28. Joachim Ritter, "Aristoteles und die Vorsokratiker," 31 [= 49].

29. C. S. Lewis, *Christian Behavior* (London 1943), 16 [= *Mere Christianity* (New York, 1952), 78]: "As Dr. Johnson said, 'People need to be reminded more often than they need to be instructed'." [*The Yale Edition of the Works of Samuel Johnson*, Volume III: *The Rambler*, Number 2 (March 24, 1750), 14, on reasons why "though it should happen that an author is capable of excelling, yet his merit may pass without notice": "What is new is opposed, because most are unwilling to be taught; and what is known is rejected, because it is not sufficiently considered, that men more frequently require to be reminded than informed."]

CHAPTER 3

1. *Goethes Farbenlehre*, G. Ipsen, ed., (Insel Verlag: Leipzig, n.d.), 553 [= *Goethes Werke*, Weimarer Ausgabe, II.3 (Weimar, 1893), 145 = Hamburger Ausgabe, Dorothea Kuhn, ed., 14 (Hamburg, 1960), 56].

2. Karl Jaspers, *Philosophie* (Berlin/Göttingen/Heidelberg, 1948), 263 [= *Philosophy* I (Chicago, 1969), 307]. Tradition is called "one form of authority" also by Hans-Georg Gadamer, *Wahrheit und Methode* (Tübingen, 1965²), 264 [= *Truth and Method* (New York, 1975), 249].

3. Theodor W. Adorno, *Ohne Leitbild. Parva Aesthetica* (Franfurt am Main, 1967), 29 [= Gesammelte Schriften 10.1 (Frankfurt am Main, 2003), 210 = "On Tradition" *Telos* 94 (Winter 1993–94), 75].

4. On this see Hans-Georg Gadamer, *Wahrheit und Methode*, 261 [= *Truth and Method*, 246].

5. Jaspers, *Philosophie*, 265 [= *Philosophy* I.309].

6. Josef Pieper, *Begriff der Tradition*, 52.

7. *Laws* 881a2.

8. *Phaedrus* 274c1.

9. Joachim Ritter, "Aristoteles und die Vorsokratiker," 25 [= 44].

10. *Meno* 81b1.

11. *Vorlesungen über die Geschichte der Philosophie*, J. Hoffmeister, ed., I (Leipzig, 1940), 6 [= *Introduction to the Lectures on the History of Philosophy*, translated by T. M. Knox and A. V. Miller (Oxford, 1985), 5].

12. It seems to me symptomatic that [Otto] Apelt's "Platon-Index" (Leipzig, 1923²), [4], cites only one passage (*Philebus* 16c), while it is easy to enumerate thirty. In this regard the (unpublished) research of Heinrich Rumphorst, "Überlieferung bei Platon" (1953), written while he was a student in Berlin, was useful to me.

13. See Karl Reinhardt's article on Posidonius in *Pauly-Wissowa, Real-Encyclopädie der classischen Altertumswissenschaft* 22.1 (1956), 572.

14. See Thomas Aquinas, *Summa theologica* I.47 [= *Opera Omnia* 4 (Rome, 1888), 485–89] and *Compendium theologiae* I.102 [= *Opera Omnia* 42 (Rome, 1979), 118–19 = *Compendium of Theology*, translated by Cyril Vollert (St. Louis, 1947), 105–6].

15. *Philebus* 16c5–9.

16. There is both in general usage and in Plato's a broader concept, in which the expression the "ancients" includes all the minds of the past, whose thinking and teaching have been especially nourished by the tradition of truth that goes back to the divine origin. See on this topic Josef Pieper, *Was heißt Akademisch?* (München, 1952), 76[–84 = *Werke* 6.103–8].

17. *De legibus* 2.27.

18. Nicholas Monzel, *Die Überlieferung* (Bonn, 1950), 129, speaks of the "original recipients of revelation."

19. Jürgen Moltmann, *Theologie der Hoffnung* (München, 1965²), 272–73 [= *Theology of Hope* (New York, 1967), 295–97.]

20. Moltmann, 273 [= 296].

21. ["In the beginning," *Genesis* 1:1; "In the fullness of time," *Galatians* 4:4.]

22. Moltmann, 273 [= 297].

23. Monzel, *Überlieferung*, 129.

24. "In terms of their matter, content and object tradition and revelation . . .coincide. All that and only that which is the object of revelation is also the object of . . . tradition."

August Deneffe, *Traditionsbegriff*, 114. See also Gerhard Gloege, *Offenbarung und Überlieferung* (Hamburg, 1954), 14, 27, 40.

25. Matthias Joseph Scheeben, *Handbuch der katholischen Dogmatik* I (Freiburg im Breisgau, 1948), 44 (§ 61) [cf. Joseph Wilhelm and Thomas B. Scannell, *A Manual of Catholic Theology Based on Scheeben's "Dogmatik"* I (London, 1909), 17: "The Catholic theory is a logical consequence of the nature of Revelation." Pieper writes "*die einfach konsequente Entwickung*," "the purely logical development"; Scheeben wrote, "*die einfache, konsequente Entwicklung*," "the simple, logically consistent development"].

26. Heinrich Scholz, *Religionsphilosophie* (Berlin, 1921), 269.

27. *Timaeus* 29d.

28. *Laws* 715e.

29. *Philebus* 30d.

30. *Metaphysics* 1074b1.

31. Moltmann, *Theology der Hoffnung*, 272 [= *Theology of Hope*, 297].

32. *Summa theologica* II, II, 2, 7 ad 3 [= *Opera Omnia* 8 (Rome, 1895), 35; *fide implicita* means with a faith that is implicit, though not explicit].

CHAPTER 4

1. Gadamer, *Wahrheit und Methode*, 265 [= *Truth and Method*, 249].

2. [The *Wandervogel* (Bird of Passage) movement was the first wave of a number of German youth movements before and after World War I that repudiated *Wilhelminismus* (the German equivalent of Victorianism) and bourgeois attitudes for a return to nature, literally, by hiking and camping in the woods, and figuratively, by a rejection of various conventions. Pieper describes his postwar participation in the movement in chapter 3 of *Noch Wußte Es Niemand*, 40–67 = *No One Could Have Known*, 37–60 = *Werke* EB 2. 51–74. For brief descriptions of the movement with bibliography see Armin Mohler, *Die Konservative Revolution in Deutschland* 1918–1932 (Stuttgart, 1950; Darmstadt, 1994[4]), 31–32, 210, 266–67, 300–304, 327–31; *Ergänzungsband* (1989) 88; John McCole, *Walter Benjamin and the Antinomies of Tradition* (Ithaca, NY, 1993), 36–41.]

3. *Summa theologica* I, II, 97.2 [= *Opera Omnia* 7 (Rome, 1892), 190 = *Treatise on Law*, R. J. Henle, ed., (Notre Dame, IN, 1993), 348–53].

4. [Martin Luther King, Jr, *Why We Can't Wait* (New York, 1964) contains the famous "Letter from Birmingham Jail." Pieper tells about his 1956 interview by the Chicago *Daily News* in *Noch Nicht Aller Tage Abend* (München, 1979), 168–69 = *Werke* EB 2.372. His visits to New Orleans under segregation (1950) and later (1956 and 1968)

are recounted in *Noch Nicht*, 180–82 = *Werke* EB 2.382–85 and *Eine Geschichte wie ein Strahl* (München, 1988), 84–88 = *Werke* EB 2.562–65. His description of King's assassination and its aftermath is in *Eine Geschichte*, 77–83 = *Werke* EB 2.556–61.]

5. [The school is the Gymnasium Paulinum or Schola Paulina in Münster. Pieper describes his schooldays there in chapters 2 and 3 of *Noch Wußte Es Nie*mand, 32–54 = *No One Could Have Known*, 30–49 = *Werke* EB 2.45–63. He mentions the parade in horse-drawn carriages, 32 = 30 = 45. Pieper's panegyric on his school, "About what is truly worth conserving," *Tradition als Herausforderung*, 48–66 = *Werke* 8.165–76, contains his most explicit defense of Latin and the classical curriculum.]

6. Monzel, *Überlieferung*, 128.

7. "Kulturtradition und Kulturkritik," 309.

8. Jean Rimaud, *Thomisme et méthode* (Paris 1925) XXXVII.

9. Yves Congar, *The Meaning of Tradition* (New York, 1964). [The first chapter (pp. 14–47) is titled "Tradition and Traditions."]

10. *Licet locus ab auctoritate, quae fundatur super ratione humana, sit infirmissimus, locus ab auctoritate, quae fundatur super revelatione divina, est efficacissimus.* Thomas Aquinas, *Summa theologica* I, 1, 8 ad 2 [= *Opera Omnia* 4 (Rome, 1888), 22].

11. *Gorgias* 522 ff.

12. *Gorgias* 525d; 526c.

13. [Pieper recounts his 1962 trip to India in chapters 13 and 14 of *Noch Nicht Aller Tage Abend*, 223–72 = *Werke* EB 2.420–64. He compares Sanskrit Departments and missions, 228–29 = *Werke* EB 2.425–26.]

14. *Republic* 621c1. More in Josef Pieper, *Über die platonischen Mythen* (München, 1965), 24–26 [= *Werke* 1.340–42].

15. See my discussion with Joseph Ratzinger after his speech, "Das Problem der Dogmengeschichte in der Sicht der katholischen Theologie," (Köln/Opladen, 1966), 35–39, 42–44 [= *Werke* 7.167–70]).

16. "The religious man does not believe in dogmas, but in God." Monzel, *Überlieferung*, 135.

CHAPTER 5

1. Deneffe, *Traditionsbegriff*, 1.

2. I refer to John Henry Newman, *Grammar of Assent* (London, 1892), 431 [= I. T. Ker, ed., (Oxford, 1985), 277].

3. Augustine, *Retractationes* I.12.

4. Deneffe, *Traditionsbegriff*, 114.

5. [Leopold Ziegler (1881–1958) wrote books that found spiritual significance in world mythology. In some respects like the American Joseph Campbell (1904–87), Ziegler displayed greater respect for Christianity.]

6. Hegel, *Vorlesungen über die Geschichte der Philosophie*, I.170 [= Knox-Miller, 125].

7. See Josef Pieper, *Über die platonischen Mythen*, 25, 86–87 [= Werke 1.340–41].

8. Thus Karl Prümm, *Der christliche Glaube und die altheidnische Welt* [I] (Leipzig, 1935), 47.

9. *Seventh Epistle* 335a3–4.

10. *Republic* 611d.

11. *Politicus* 290b.

12. Paul Friedländer, *Platon* I (Berlin 1954) 184 [= *Plato: An Introduc*tion (New York, 1958), 173].

13. M. J. Scheeben, *Handbuch der katholischen Dogmatik* I [(Freiburg, 1948)], 291 (§ 633). [Wilhelm and Scannell do not summarize this passage, but they translate a similar one about the believer and God: "Grace makes this connection so perfect that a most intimate union and relationship are established between the believer's knowledge and the Divine knowledge." (*Dogmatik* I.301 (§ 660) = *Manual* I.117).]

14. John Henry Newman, [*Fifteen Sermons Preached before the University of Oxford between A. D. 1826 and 1843* (London, 1909), 236; often referred to as *Oxford University Sermons* = *Fifteen Sermons*, James David Earnest and Gerard Tracey, eds. (Oxford, 2006), 163.]

15. *Philosophie*, 259 [= *Philosophy* I.303].

16. G. Gloege, *Offenbarung und Überlieferung*, 27.

17. V. Iwanow, *Das Alte Wahre*, 33 [= Viacheslav Ivanov, *Selected Essays* (Evanston, IL, 2001), 145].

18. See *Apologeticum* 46; *De praescriptione haereticorum* 7.

19. Carl Gustav Jung, *Psychologie und Religion* (Zürich/Leipzig, 1940), 76 [= *Psychology and Religion* (New Haven, CT, 1938), 49. Jung calls an "insight . . . which consciousness has not been able to produce" intuition.].

20. Jung, 93 [= 64. Jung calls these "preconscious, primordial ideas" archetypes, 93 = 63.].

21. Jung, 93 [= 64. "The archetypal motives . . . are not only transmitted by tradition and migration but also by heredity."].

22. Étienne Gilson, *The Christian Philosophy of Saint Augustine* (New York, 1960), 299–300.

23. See *Confessions* X.20.

24. *Phaedrus* 244b6.

25. Gabriel Marcel, *Das Grosse Erbe* (Münster, 1952), 29.

26. Joseph Ratzinger, "Problem der Dogmengeschichte," 44.

27. Marcel 22, 24.

28. Jaspers, *Von der Wahrheit*, 192.

29. *De vegetabilibus* [6.1.1 §1], C. Jessen, ed. (Berlin, 1867), 340. See also Josef Pieper, *Scholastik* (München, 1960), 157–60 [= *Scholasticism. Personalities and Problems of Medieval Philosophy* (New York, 1960), 115–18 = *Werke* 2.394–97. For problems with this passage, see my "Reflections," VI.]

30. Joachim Ritter does this in Josef Pieper, *Begriff der Tradition*, 45–46.

CHAPTER 6

1. J. Ritter in Josef Piper, *Begriff der Tradition*, 47.

2. 983a5–10. See the commentary of William David Ross, *Aristotle's Metaphysics* I (Oxford, 1924), 121.

3. "Tradition is never simply the restraining counterforce; it is always resistance and progress at the same time." Theodor Litt, "Hegels Begriff des Geistes und das Problem der Tradition," *Studium Generale* 4 (1951), 320.

4. Odo Marquard, *Skeptische Methode im Blick auf Kant* (Freiburg/München, 1958), 77, attributed this silly opinion to me, invoking one of my writings, where he could have read the following sentence: "Strictly speaking, the philosophizer, while he is philosophizing, is neither handing down tradition nor interpreting tradition." (*Begriff der Tradition*, 54)

5. See Josef Pieper, *Verteidigungsrede für de Philosophie* (München, 1966), 14 [–25 = *In Defence of Philosophy* (San Francisco, 1992), 12–21 = *Werke* 3.79–86].

6. Thomas Aquinas, *Commentary on Aristotle's "On Heaven and Earth"* I.22 [= *Opera Omnia* 3 (Rome, 1886), 91].

7. *Gesammelte Werke*. Musarion-Aufgabe 18 (München, 1926), 56 [= *Werke in drei Bänden*, Karl Schlechta, ed., 3 (München, 1956), 644–45 = *The Will to Power*, translated by Walter Kaufmann and H. J. Hollingdale (New York, 1967), 43. The note is dated Nov. 1887–March 1888 by Otto Weiss, Musarion 19, 418, because he placed it in notebook W XI (= W II 3), 57, which Nietzsche wrote in between those dates, Nietzsche's Werke 16 (Leipzig, 1911), 482. Schlechta agrees with Weiss. Giorgio Colli and Mazzino Montinari report this aphorism as the first paragraph of a fair copy

of *Twilight of the Idols* 39, found in notebook W II 6 and transcribed at Friedrich Nietzsche, *Kritische Studienausgabe* (KSA) 14 (Munich, 1988), 431–32. Nietzsche delivered the fair copy of *Twilight* to his publisher, September 7, 1888.]

8. Letter of March 18, 1811 [= *Goethes Werke*. Weimarer Ausgabe IV.22 (Weimar, 1901), 68 = *Goethe's Letters to Zelter*, translated by A. D. Coleridge (London, 1887), 81. Although Adrian Del Caro has persuaded me that the passage can mean that every artist has to struggle against his age, I still suspect a misprint here and that Goethe meant "Dieses Jahrhundert aber," "This century, however . . .".].

9. *Philosophie*, 267, 269 [= *Philosophy* I.310–11, 312].

10. Karl Jaspers and Rudolf Bultmann, *Die Frage der Entmythologisierung* (München, 1954), 12 [= *Myth and Christianity* (New York, 1958), 8. Jaspers is discussing the Martin Heidegger of *Sein und Zeit* = *Being and Time*].

11. See *Das Alte Wahre*, 188. [In the *Nachwort*, or epilogue, to this book, Victor Wittkowski calls Ivanov "this Russian Westerner," because he participates in the tradition of European humanism.]

12. Vyacheslav Ivanovich Ivanov and Mikhail Osipovich Gershenzon, *Correspondence across a Room* (Marlboro, VT, 1984), 4–5.

13. Ivanov and Gershenzon, 61.

14. A somewhat unexpected confirmation of this opinion is found in Leszek Kolakowski, "Von Sinn der Tradition," 1092 [=15 = 46]: "If it should happen—which fortunately is not likely—that the opposition to tradition should lead to its complete rejection, we would be absolutely correct to speak of the end of the humane world."

15. *Geschichte und Tradition*, 28 [= 94].

BIBLIOGRAPHY

BOOKS MENTIONED IN TEXT AND NOTES OF *TRADITION*

Adorno, Theodor W., *Ohne Leitbild. Parva Aesthetica* (Frankfurt am Main, 1967).

———, *Gesammelte Schriften* 10.1: *Kulkturkritik und Gesellschaft* I (Frankfurt am Main, 2003).

Albertus Magnus, *De Animalibus Libri XXVI.* Hermann Stadler, ed., 2 vols. (Munster, 1916–20).

———, *De vegetabilibus libri VII*, Carolus Jessen, ed., (Berlin, 1867).

———, *On Animals. A Medieval* Summa Zoologica, translated and annotated by Kenneth F. Kitchell and Irven Michael Resenick, 2 vols. (Baltimore, 1999).

Apelt, Otto, *Platon-Index als Gesamtregister zu der Übersetzung in der Philosophischen Bibliothek*, Band 182 (Leipzig, 1923^2).

Bacher, Wilhelm, *Tradition und Tradenten in den Schulen in Palästinas und Baby*loniens (Leipzig, 1914).

Barrow, John D., *The Book of Nothing: Vacuums, Voids, and the Latest Ideas about the Origins of the Universe* (New York/London, 2000).

———, *The World within the World* (Oxford, 1988).

Brugger, Walter, ed., *Philosophical Dictionary*, translated by Kenneth Baker (Spokane, WA, 1972).

Congar, Yves, *The Meaning of Tradition* (New York, 1964).

Deneffe, August, *Der Traditionsbegriff: Studie zur Theologie* (Münster in Westfalen, 1931).

Descartes, René, *Œuvres*, Charles Adam and Paul Tannery, edd., VI: *Discours de la Méthode & Essais* (Paris, 1902).

———, VIIIA: *Principia Philosophiae* (Paris, 1905).

———, *Philosophical Writings of Descartes*, translated by John Cottingham, Robert Stoothoff, and Dugald Murdoch, 3 vols. (Cambridge, 1985).

Einstein, Albert, Hedwig und Max Born, *Briefwechsel 1916–1955* (München, 1969).

———, *The Born-Einstein Letters: Friendship, Politics and Physics in Uncertain Times* (Basingstoke–New York, 1972, 2005²).

Eisler, Rudolf, ed., *Wörterbuch der philosophischen Begriffe und Ausdrücke* (Berlin, 1899).

Fleming, Thomas, *The Politics of Human Nature* (New Brunswick, NJ, 1988).

Friedländer, Paul, *Plato: An Introduction* (New York, 1958).

———, *Platon* I: *Seinswahrheit und Lebenswirklichkeit* (Berlin, 1954²).

Gadamer, Hans-Georg, *Die Aktualität des Schönen* (Stuttgart, 1977).

———, *The Relevance of the Beautiful and Other Essays*, translated by Nicholas Walker (Cambridge, 1986).

———, *Truth and Method* (New York, 1975; 1989²).

———, *Wahrheit und Methode: Grundzüge einer philosophischen Hermeneutik* (Tübingen, 1960; 1965²; 1972³).

Gilson, Étienne, *The Christian Philosophy of Saint Augustine* (New York, 1960).

Gloege, Gerhard, *Offenbarung und Überlieferung: Ein dogmatische Entwurf* (Hamburg, 1954).

Goethe, Johann Wolfgang, *Goethes Farbenlehre*, Gunther Ipsen, ed., (Leipzig, n.d. [1926]).

———, *Goethe's Letters to Zelter*, translated by A. D. Coleridge (London, 1887).

———, *Goethes Werke.* Hamburger Ausgabe, *Wissenschaftliche Schriften* (Zweiter Teil), Dorothea Kuhn, ed., XIV (Hamburg, 1960).

———, Goethes Werke. Weimarer Ausgabe, IV. Abteilung: *Goethes Briefe*, 22 (Januär 1811–April 1812) (Weimar, 1901).

Grant, Edward, *Much Ado about Nothing: Theories of Space and Vacuum from the Middle Ages to the Scientific Revolution* (Cambridge, 1981).

Hegel, G. F. W., *Introduction to the Lectures on the History of Philosophy*, translated by T. M. Knox and A. V. Miller (Oxford, 1985).

———, *Lectures on the Philosophy of World History: Introduction: Reason in History*, translated by H. B. Nisbet (Cambridge, 1975).

———, *Vorlesungen über die Geschichte der Philosophie* I, Johannes Hoffmeister ed., *Sämtliche Werke*, kritische Ausgabe XVA (Leipzig, 1940).

———, *Vorlesungen über die Philosophie der Weltgeschichte* I: *Einleitung*: *Die Vernunft in der Geschichte*, Johnnes Hoffmeister, ed., Sämtliche Werke, neue kritische Ausgabe XVIIIA (Leipzig, 1955).

Heisenberg, Werner, *Tradition in Science* (New York, 1975).

Hoffmeister, Johannes, *Wörterbuch der philosophischen Begriffe* (Hamburg, 1955²).

Horkheimer, Max and Theodor W. Adorno, *Dialectic of Enlightenment* (New York, 1972).

———, *Dialektik der Aufklärung* (Amsterdam, 1947).

Ivanov, Viacheslav, *Selected Essays* (Evanston, IL, 2001).

Ivanov, Vyacheslav Ivanovich and Mikhail Osipovich Gershenzon, *Correspondence across a Room*, translated by Lisa Sergio (Marlboro, VT, 1984).

Iwanow, Wjatscheslaw, *Das Alte Wahre. Essays* (Frankfurt am Main, 1954).

Jaeger, Werner, *Aristoteles. Grundlegung einer Geschichte seiner Entwicklung* (Berlin, 1923).

———, *Aristotle. Fundamentals of the History of his Development* (Oxford, 1934).

Jaspers, Karl, *Philosophie* (Berlin/Göttingen/Heidelberg, 1948²).

———, *Philosophy*, 3 vols. (Chicago, 1969).

———, *Über die Wahrheit* (München, 1947).

Jaspers, Karl and Rudolf Bultmann, *Die Frage der Entmythologisierung* (München, 1954).

———, *Myth and Christianity* (New York, 1958).

Johnson, Samuel, *The Yale Edition of the Works of Samuel Johnson*, 3: *The Rambler* (New Haven/London, 1969).

Jung, Carl Gustav, *Psychologie und Religion* (Zürich/Leipzig, 1940).

———, *Psychology and Religion* (New Haven, CT, 1938).

Jünger, Ernst, *Der Arbeiter. Herrschaft und Gestalt* (Hamburg, 1932; Stuttgart, 1981).

Kahn, Charles H. *Pythagoras and the Pythagoreans* (Indianapolis, 2001).

Kant, Immanuel, *Correspondence*. Translated and Edited by Arnulf Zweig (Cambridge, 1999).

———, *Kant's gesammelte Schriften* XI (Berlin/Leipzig).

———, *Kant's gesammelte Schriften* XXIII: *Kant's Handschriftlicher Nachlaß* (Berlin, 1955).

———, *Kant. Philosophical Correspondence 1759-99*, edited and translated by Arnulf Zweig (Chicago, 1967).

King, Martin Luther, Jr., *Why We Can't Wait* (New York, 1964).

Kirk, G. S., J. E. Raven, and M. Schofield, *The Pre-Socratic Philosophers* (Cambridge, 1983²).

Kittel, Gerhard, ed., *Theological Dictionary of the New Testament*, translated by Geoffrey W. Bromily, 2 (Grand Rapids, MI, 1964).

———, *Theologisches Wörterbuch zum Neuen Testament* 2 (Stuttgart, 1935).

Krüger, Gerhard, *Freiheit und Weltverwaltigung. Aufsätze zur Philosophie der Geschichte* (Freiburg/München, 1958).

———, *Geschichte und Tradition* (Stuttgart, 1948).

Kullmann,Wolfgang, *Aristoteles und die moderne Wissenschaft* (Stuttgart, 1998).

———, *Wissenschaft und Methode* (Berlin, 1974).

Lewis, C. S., *Christian Behavior* (London, 1943).

———, *Mere Christianity* (New York, 1952).

———, *Über den Schmerz* (mit einem Nachwort von Josef Pieper) (Köln, 1954).

Lutz, Christopher Stephen, *Tradition in the Ethics of Alasdair MacIntyre* (Lanham, MD, 2004).

MacIntyre, Alasdair, *After Virtue: A Study in Moral Theory* (Notre Dame, IN, 1981, 1984²).

———, *Whose Justice? Which Rationality?* (Notre Dame, IN, 1988).

———, *Three Rival Versions of Moral Inquiry: Encyclopaedia, Genealogy and Tradition* (Notre Dame, IN, 1990).

Marcel, Gabriel, *Das Große Erbe* (Münster, 1952).

Marquard, Odo, *Skeptische Methode im Blick auf Kant* (Freiburg/München, 1958).

McCole, John, *Walter Benjamin and the Antinomies of Tradition* (Ithaca, NY, 1993).

Mohler, Armin, *Die Konservative Revolution in Deutschland 1918-1932. Ein Handbuch* (Stuttgart, 1950; Darmstadt, 1994⁴).

Moltmann, Jurgen, *Theologie der Hoffnung* (München, 1965²).

———, *Theology of Hope: On the Ground and the Implications of a Christian Eschatology* (New York, 1967).

Monzel, Nikolaus, *Die Überlieferung. Phänomenologische und religionssoziologische Untersuchungen über den Traditionalismus der christlichen Lehre* (Bonn, 1950).

Neusner, Jacob, *The Talmud of Babylonia: An Academic Commentary*, V: *Yoma* (Atlanta, 1994).

Newman, John Henry, *Essay in Aid of a Grammar of Assent*, I. T. Ker, ed. (Oxford, 1985).

———, *Fifteen Sermons Preached before the University of Oxford between A.D. 1826 and 1843* (London, 1872).

———, *Fifteen Sermons Preached before the University of Oxford between A.D. 1826 and 1843*, James David Earnest and Gerard Tracey, eds. (Oxford, 2006).

Newton, Isaac, *Philosophiae Naturalis Principia Mathematica* (Cambridge, MA, 1972).

———, *The Principia* (Berkeley, CA, 1999).

Nietzsche, Friedrich, *Gesammelte Werke* (Musarionausgabe), 18 (München, 1926): *Der Wille zur Macht. Versuch einer Umwertung aller Werthe.* Erstes und Zweites Buch.

———, *Nietzsche's Werke* (Groß Oktavausgabe), *Ecce Homo. Der Wille zur Macht* 15–16 (Leipzig, 1911).

———, *Werke in drei Bänden*, Karl Schlechta, ed. (München, 1956).

———, *The Will to Power*, translated by Walter Kaufmann and H. J. Hollingdale (New York, 1967).

Owen, G. E. L., *Logic, Scientific and Dialectic: Collected Papers* (Ithaca, NY, 1986).

Pascal, Blaise, *Great Shorter Writings of Pascal*, translated by Emile Cailliet and John C. Blankenagel (Philadelphia, 1948).

———, *Œuvres*, Léon Brunschvicg et Pierre Boutroux, eds., II (Paris, 1908).

———, *Œuvres Complètes*, Louis Lafuma, ed. (Paris, 1963).

———, *Œuvres Complètes*, Michel Le Guern, ed., I (Paris, 1998).

Pauly, August Friedrich von, Georg Wissowa and Konrat Ziegler, *Paulys Real-Encyclopädie der classischen Altertumswissenschaften*, 1–47 (Stuttgart, 1894–1963); II.1–19 (Stuttgart, 1914–72).

Pieper, Josef, *Belief and Faith: A Philosophical Tract* (New York, 1963).

———, *Eine Geschichte wie ein Strahl. Autobiographische Aufzeichnungen seit 1964* (München, 1988).

———, *For the Love of Wisdom: Essays on the Nature of Philosophy.* Edited by Berthold Wald, translated by Roger Wasserman (San Francisco, 2006).

———, *Fortitude and Temperance* (New York, 1954).

———, *In Defense of Philosophy* (San Francisco, 1992).

———, *Leisure: The Basis of Culture* (New York, 1952).

———, *Muße und Kult* (München, 1948).

———, *Neuordnung der menschlichen Gesellschaft: Befreiung des Proletariats/ Berufständische Gliederung, Systematische Einführung in die Enzyklika* Quadragesimo Anno (Frankfurt am Main, 1932).

————, *Noch Nicht Aller Tage Abend. Autobiographische Aufzeichnungen 1945–1964* (München, 1979).

————, *Noch Wußte Es Niemand. Autobiographische Aufzeichnungen 1904–1945* (München, 1976).

————, *No One Could Have Known. An Autobiography: The Early Years 1904–1945* (San Francisco, 1987).

————, *Problems of Modern Faith* (Chicago, 1984).

————, *Scholasticism: Personalities and Problems of Medieval Philosophy* (New York, 1960).

————, *"Scholastik": Gestalten und Probleme der mittelalterlichen Philosophie* (München, 1960).

————, *The End of Time: A Meditation on the Philosophy of History* (New York, 1954).

————, *Tradition als Herausforderung* (München, 1963).

————, *Über das Ende der Zeit* (München, 1950).

————, *Über den Begriff der Tradition* (Köln/Opladen, 1958).

————, *Über den Glauben. Ein philosophischer Traktat* (München, 1962).

————, *Über den platonischen Mythen* (München, 1965).

————, *Über die Schwierigkeit, heute zu glauben* (München, 1974).

————, *Überlieferung. Begriff und Anspruch* (München, 1970).

————, *Verteidigungsrede für die Philosophie* (München, 1966).

————, *Was heißt Akademisch? oder der Funkionär und der Sophist* (München, 1952).

————, *Was heißt Philosophieren?* (München, 1948).

————, *Werke in acht Bänden* (+ 2 Ergänzungsbände), Berthold Wald, ed., (Hamburg, 1995–2005).

————, 1: *Darstellungen und Interpretationen: Platon* (Hamburg, 2002).

————, 2: *Darstellungen und Interpretationen: Thomas von Aquin und die Scholastik* (Hamburg, 2001).

————, 3: *Schriften zum Philosophiebegriff* (Hamburg, 1995).

————, 4: *Schriften zur Philosophischen Anthropologie und Ethik: Das Menschenbild der Tugendlehre* (Hamburg, 1996).

————, 5: *Schriften zur Philosophischen Anthropologie und Ethik: Grundstrukturen menschlicher Existenz* (Hamburg, 1997).

————, 6: *Kulturphilosophische Schriften* (Hamburg, 1999).

————, 7: *Religionsphilosophische Schriften* (Hamburg, 2000).

————, 8.1: *Miszellen* (Hamburg, 2005).

————, 8.1: *Register und Gesamtbibliographie* (Hamburg, 2007).

————, Ergänzungsband 1: *Frühe soziologische Schriften* (Hamburg, 2004).

————, Ergänzungsband 2: *Autobiographische Schriften* (Hamburg, 2005).

————, *Von Sinn der Tapferkeit* (Leipzig, 1934).

Polanyi,Michael, *Science, Faith, and Society*, Riddell Memorial Lectures, Eighteenth Series (London, 1946).

Pongratz, L. J., ed., *Philosophie in Selbstdarstellungen* I (Hamburg, 1975).

Popper, Karl, *Conjectures and Refutations* (London, 1962).

Prümm, Karl, *Der christliche Glaube und die altheidnische Welt* I–II (Leipzig, 1935).

Ratzinger, Joseph, *Das Problem der Dogmengeschichte in der Sicht der katholischen Theologie* (Köln/Opladen, 1966).

Rawls, John, *A Theory of Justice* (Cambridge, MA, 1971).

Reinisch, Leonhard, ed., *Vom Sinn der Tradition* (München, 1970).

Rimaud, Jean, *Thomisme et méthode* (Paris, 1925).

Rist, John M., *On Inoculating Moral Philosophy against God* (Milwaukee, 1999).

Ritter, Joachim and Karlfried Gründer, edd., *Historisches Wörterbuch der Philosophie*, I–XII (Basel, 1971–98).

Ritter, Joachim, *Metaphysik und Politik. Studien zu Aristoteles und Hegel* (Frankfurt am Main, 1969).

Ross, William David, *Aristotle's Metaphysics* I–II (Oxford, 1924).

Rumphorst, Heinrich, *Überlieferung bei Platon* (unpublished Berlin dissertation, 1953).

Schatz, Otto, ed., *Was Wird aus dem Menschen* (Graz/Wien/ Köln, 1974).

Scheeben, Matthias Joseph, *Handbuch der katholischen Dogmatik* I–II (Freiburg im Breisgau, 1948).

Schmitt, Arbogast, *Die Moderne und Platon* (Stuttgart, 2003).

Scholtz, Heinrich, *Religionsphilosophie* (Berlin, 1921).

Shils, Edward, *Tradition* (London, 1981).

Sohm, Rudolph, *Institutionen. Geschichte und System des römischen Privatrechts* (Leipzig, 1905[12]).

————, *The Institutes: A Textbook of the History and System of Roman Private Law*, translated by James Crawford Ledlie (Oxford, 1907[3]).

Soloviev, V. S., *Heart of Reality: Essays on Beauty, Love, and Ethics* (Notre Dame, IN, 2003).

Taylor, Charles, *A Catholic Modernity: Charles Taylor's Marianist Award Lecture* (New York/Oxford, 1999).

———, *Hegel* (Cambridge, 1975).

Thomas Aquinas, *Commentary on Aristotle's Physics*, translated by Richard J. Blackwell, Richard J. Spath and W. Edmund Thirkel (New Haven, CT, 1963).

———, *Compendium of Theology*, translated by Cyril Vollert (St. Louis/London, 1947).

———, *Opera Omnia iussu impensaque Leonis XIII P. M. edita, Commentaria in octo libros Physicorum Aristotelis*, 2 (Rome, 1984).

———, *Commentaria in libros Aristotelis De caelo et mundo*, 3 (Rome, 1886).

———, *Summa Theologiae*, 4–12 (Rome, 1888–1906).

———, *Compendium Theologiae* etc., 42 (Rome, 1979).

———, *Summa Theologiae*, Pietro Caramello et al., eds., I–IV (Turin/Rome, 1948–50).

———, *The Treatise on Law* [Being *Summa Theologiae*, I–II, QQ. 90 through 97], R. J. Henle, ed., (Notre Dame, IN, 1993).

Thorndike, Lynn, *A History of Magic and Experimental Science During the First Thirteen Centuries of Our Era*, II (New York and London, 1923).

Vulliaud, Paul, *Le clé traditionelle des Évangiles* (Paris, 1936).

Westfall, Richard S., *The Construction of Modern Science: Mechanisms and Mechanics* (London, 1971; Cambridge, 1977).

Wigner, Eugene, *Symmetries and Reflections* (Bloomington, IN, 1967).

Wilhelm, Joseph, and Thomas B. Scannell, *A Manual of Catholic Theology Based on Scheeben's "Dogmatik,"* I–II (London, 1908–9).

Ziegler, Leopold, *Menschwerdung*, 2 vols. (Olten, 1947).

ARTICLES MENTIONED IN TEXT AND NOTES OF *TRADITION*

Adorno, Theodor W., "On Tradition," *Telos* 94 (Winter 1993), 75–81.

Büchsel, Friedrich, "Paradosis," *Theological Dictionary of the New Testament* II (Grand Rapids, MI, 1964).

Ehrhardt, Arnold, "Traditio," *Paulys Real-Encyclopädie der classischen Altertumswissenschaften* II.6 (1937), 1875–92.

Fleming, Thomas, "Homage to T. S. Eliot," *Chronicles* 12.4 (April 1988), 8–9.

Heisenberg, Werner, "Tradition in Science," *Tradition in Science* (New York, 1975).

Kolokowski, Lezcek, "Der Anspruch auf die selbstverschuldete Unmündigkeit," in Leonhard Reinisch, ed., *Von Sinn der Tradition* (München, 1970), 1–15.

————, "On the Meaning of Tradition," *Evergreen Review* v. 15, no. 88 (April 1971), 43–46.

————, "Von Sinn der Tradition," *Merkur 23*.12 (December 1969), 1085–92.

Krüger, Gerhard, "Die Bedeutung der Tradition für die philosophische Forschung," *Studium Generale* 4 (1951), 321–28.

Litt, Theodor, "Hegels Begriff des Geistes und das Problem der Tradition," *Studium Generale* 4 (1951), 311–21.

Pieper, Josef, "Das Gesellschaftsideal in der industriellen Arbeitswelt. Aufriß einer sozialpädagogischen Grundfrage," *Pharus* 25 (1934), 268-78.

————, "On Clarity," *Chronicles* 12.4 (April 1988), 12–13.

Karl Popper, "Towards a Rational Theory of Tradition," *Rationalist Annual* (1949), 36–55.

————, *Conjectures and Refutations* (London, 1962), 120–35.

Reinhardt, Karl, "Posidonios (3)," *Paulys Real-Encyclopädie der classischen Altertumswissenschaften* 22.1 (1953), 558–826.

Ritter, Joachim, "Aristoteles und die Vorsokratiker," *Felsefi Arkivi* [Istanbul] 3 (1954) 17–37.

————, *Metaphysik und Politik. Studien zu Aristoteles und Hegel* (Frankfurt am Main, 1969), 34–56.

Rüstow, Alexander, "Kulturtradition und Kulturkritik," *Studium Generale* 4 (1951), 307–11.

Steenblock, Volker, "Tradition," *Historisches Wörterbuch der Philosophie*, 10 (Basel, 1998), 1315–29.

Taylor, Charles, "Geschlossene Weltstrukturen in der Moderne," *Wissen und Weisheit* (Dokumentationen der Josef Pieper Stiftung, Band 6) (Münster, 2005), 137–69.

Wigner, Eugene, "The Unreasonable Effectiveness of Mathematics in the Natural Sciences," *Communications in Pure and Applied Mathematics* 13.1 (February 1960).

INDEX

Pascal, Blaise, xiv, xxvii, xxx, 3–6, 25–26, 50, 59, 61

Paul of Tarsus, 11, 14

Pauly-Wissowa (*Realencyclopädie*), 7

philosophy, 59, 61–68

physics, xxvii–xxx, 5–6, 62

Plato, xviii, xxi, xxv–xxvi, xxviii–xxix, 11–12, 26–31, 33–34, 46–47, 52–53, 57, 63

    Gorgias, 11, 17, 44

    Phaedo, 27

    Philebus, 27

    Republic, 53

    Symposium, xxi, 11, 63

Polanyi, Michael, xxix

Popper, Karl, xxix

preservation, 15, 21–22, 40, 45–46, 50

progress, 1–3, 20–21, 24, 26, 41, 46, 59, 62

prophets, 29, 31

revelation, 29–32, 41, 46–47, 49–52, 54

revelation, original, 30, 34, 51, 54, 57

Rist, John M., xxv–xxvi

Roman law, 7

Rüstow, Alexander, 19, 41

sacred tradition, xix–xxi, xxv–xxviii, xxx–xxxi, 21, 31–35, 37, 39–43, 45, 47, 49–57, 59, 61–68

Sartre, Jean-Paul, xxi, 44, 64, 66

Schmitt, Arbogast, xxvi

science, xxvi–xxxi, 59, 62, 68

"scientific philosophy," 66

Shils, Edward, xxix

Socrates, 11, 17–18, 27, 31, 44, 52–54, 63

Steenblock, Volker, 75

Taylor, Charles, xxi–xxii

Tertullian, 54

theology, xxvii–xxx, 5–6, 28, 31, 45–47, 61–62

traditionalism, 6, 57

traditional customs, 35–38

tradition, break with, loss of, 16, 40, 42, 59

translation, tradition as, 45, 50

Transmettre, 13

unity of mankind, 68

vacuum, void, xiv, 3–5, 74, 86

Wandervogel, 38

Wigner, Eugene, xxviii

words, careless use of, 13

Ziegler, Leopold, 52

ABOUT THE AUTHOR AND TRANSLATOR

JOSEF PIEPER (1904–97) was a popular and prolific German philosopher noted for his accessible style. Many of his books are available in English, including *The Four Cardinal Virtues, Only the Lover Sings: Art and Contemplation*, and the acclaimed and influential *Leisure: The Basis of Culture*.

E. CHRISTIAN KOPFF has taught at the University of Colorado, Boulder, since 1973, and has been associate director of the university's Honors Program since 1990. He is the editor of a critical edition of Euripides' *Bacchae* and author of over one hundred articles and reviews on scholarly, pedagogical, and popular topics.